IMAGES
of America

FRANKLIN, HAMBURG, OGDENSBURG, AND HARDYSTON

IMAGES
of America

FRANKLIN, HAMBURG, OGDENSBURG, AND HARDYSTON

William R. Truran

ARCADIA
PUBLISHING

Published by Arcadia Publishing
Charleston, South Carolina

Library of Congress Catalog Card Number: 2004106379

For all general information contact Arcadia Publishing at:
Telephone 843-853-2070
Fax 843-853-0044
E-mail sales@arcadiapublishing.com
For customer service and orders:
Toll-Free 1-888-313-2665

Visit us on the Internet at www.arcadiapublishing.com

On the cover: Members of the Franklin Community Club (mostly teenagers) prepare for a trip to see the Giants play football at the Polo Grounds in New York. They will return without smiles on their faces, as the date is December 7, 1941, the day Pearl Harbor was attacked. Shown kneeling in the first row are, from left to right, Ken Manuel, Tom Butto, Joe Milak, and Billy Glynn. Standing in the back row are, from left to right, Charlie Ora, Charles Olah, Willie Kasisky, Steve Stefkovich, Paul Barta, Moon Kinney, Joe Kisac, Andy Donche, and Ed Stefkovich. Members of the group shown in this photograph also include John Palush, John Trichine, Hank Rutan, John Kouach, Joe Chuchwa, Steve Piniaha, Mike Kisac, Conrad Biedron, Junior Webb, Dave Mindlin, Walter Czesnowski, Ben Breznik, Charlie Fletcher, Walt Webb, Jack Glynn, Harold Toppel, Joe Garnis, Jim Moneypenny, Alex Denensewich, Martin Durachko, Ronnie Roskelly, Mike Korzuk, and Leslie Kistle. (Courtesy Franklin Historical Society.)

CONTENTS

ACKNOWLEDGMENTS

My grandfather Sydney Hall worked in the mines in Franklin from 1910 until they closed. He had a number of unique photographs that I feared would be lost forever unless they were catalogued, documented in detail, and stored in a format and place for others to enjoy and learn from. It is from the desire to preserve this passing heritage for posterity that this book was born.

This work would not have been possible without the contributions and assistance of many people and groups. In addition to the following, there are likely people whom I have inadvertently neglected to name but appreciate ever so much.

Individuals who helped include Betty and Bob Allen, Betty Banta, Harvey Barlow, Dan Barr, Jack Baum, Joe Bene, Dick and Pat Bowman, Lou Cherepy Sr. (Franklin's historian) and Lou Cherepy Jr., John Cianciulli, Louise Clark, Pete Dunn, Mary Eleanor Eppler and William Eppler (for several photographs including the two portraits of the Ogdens taken at the Governor's Mansion in Elizabeth), Frank Fasolo, Wasco and Sylvia Hadowanetz, Dick Hauck and Bob Hauck, Florence Clark Kitchell, John Kolic, Gregg Kresge, Georgeanna Lewis, Sen. Robert and Ginnie Littell, Eddie and Estelle Mindlin, Joseph P. Quinn Jr., Pauline and Georgie Riggio, Dave Rutan, Joan Bennetts Simmons, Michael and Olga Stefkovich, Nancy Littell Wesighan, Peggy Senchuck Willeford, Dr. Marion Wood (who was of exceptional assistance with *All About Hamburg*), and Helen and Bill Wurst.

Community associations that were open and extremely helpful include Franklin Historical Society, Franklin Mineral Museum, Hamburg Historical Society, Hardyston Historical Society, Sterling Mine Museum, Ogdensburg Museum, Sparta Historical Society, Carol Crowley and the Franklin Branch of the Sussex County Library system, the Fred J. Stephens collection, Edison Antiques, Denise Losty and the Bank of New York, Art Jordan and Antique Photos, Leonard DeGraff and Edison National Historical Site, and Jody and the Wilcox Press. Also, a number of the photographs in the book are by A. J. Bloom, a prominent professional photographer of the area who resided in Hamburg.

All of these individuals and groups were a delight to work with and shared a common desire to express the history of the community.

Finally, there are two others without whom I would not have been able to complete this endeavor: my mother, Stella Eva Hall Truran, who was a great help in networking with those whom she knew in the community; and my wife, Ginny Johnson Truran, who gave me her longstanding support, especially when I was squirreled away at the computer. Thank you.

INTRODUCTION

Home in the New Jersey Highlands of the Hamburg Mountains
and nestled lakes, gathering flow of the Wallkill River, mineral resources,
dairy farms, and rural home to much wildlife and people.

This book conveys the history of the highlands in northwestern New Jersey, the greater Wallkill Valley area, which includes the communities of Franklin, Ogdensburg, Hamburg, and Hardyston. Most of the images represent the valley of a century ago—impressions and reflections that in many instances are no longer here to be seen—showing life as it was and offering some insight into how it might be in the future.

The book is an overview of the area's history, not a highly detailed historical account. All of the area included is within the original Hardyston Township. Sussex County was set off from Morris County in 1753. Hardyston Township was set off from New Town in 1762, was named after the royal governor Josiah Hardy, and included at the time all of Vernon, Sparta, Ogdensburg, Franklin, and Hamburg. Hardyston Township was carved up into smaller municipalities with their own spheres of interest: Vernon on November 19, 1772; Sparta on February 13, 1845; Franklin on March 13, 1913; Ogdensburg (from Sparta) on March 31, 1914; and Hamburg on March 19, 1920.

This introduction gives a very brief description of the natural history of the valley. The four chapters that follow provide a closer look at the four towns, starting about 100 years ago and exploring how each grew and prospered, with its own railroad station, main street, lodging, businesses, industry, schools, churches, homes, and places of natural interest. Each had its own prominent citizens who devoted many years and perhaps a lifetime toward furthering the success of the town.

This journey through the Wallkill River Valley follows not the more common paths but rather the route taken by Arendt Schuyler in the late 1600s. It begins in Hardyston Township, a mountainous area with some lakes cloistered within the hilly terrain. The journey continues in the south at Ogdensburg and proceeds through Franklin Borough and over to the northern edge of Hamburg, with Hardyston Township surrounding the valley on every side but the south.

American Indians first inhabited this area of New Jersey, coming across America from Siberia near the end of the last ice age, about 10,000 years ago. The climate was much colder then, and there were numerous large animals that provided food to eat: mastodon, caribou, moose, and elk. The Indians were not numerous and were not evenly distributed. They traveled in small groups made up of related family members as clans. The more recent Woodland period Indians had dugout canoes made from tree trunks and used lodges 20 to 60 feet long, made of bent saplings lashed and covered with bark. Fairly nomadic, they moved as the game and soil conditions changed but also had shelters and rich hunting areas that they frequented over time, such as Wildcat Rock Shelter in Franklin, used by cliff dwellers up to 8000 B.C. The Lenape, or "ordinary" people, were part of the Algonquin Nation. Those here spoke the Munsee dialect and were of the rather peaceful Minisink band of the Lenape. Their pathways many times followed the easy course of the streams, and these became the first routes of the Europeans and are today some of the main roads such as Route 94.

The European settlers were probably here before 1740. As they moved in, they displaced the Indians. Early pioneers were the Dutch who were exploring for minerals, followed by early land owners or people who leased land. A few names exist on rudimentary deeds or surveys; later pioneers included the Gould and, later, the Wallings and Rorick families.

The rivers provided abundant water for crops, and the elevation provided power for later industries: the iron forges, gristmills, fulling mills, sawmills, paper mills, and distilleries beginning in the late 1700s. However, it was the richness of mineral resources that brought attention to the area. Heavy metals, such as zinc from Franklin and Ogdensburg, supplied the world for many years. Abundant iron in the earth throughout the Wallkill Valley, and literally lying on the ground in some places as bog iron, was mined for various purposes. Today, the area around Franklin remains an active source for sand and gravel used throughout northern New Jersey.

In the early 1700s, pioneers (including many Dutch) came probably southwest from Kingston and Ulster County, New York, via the Wallkill River. In the late 1700s, due to conditions in Morris County after the Revolution, many Morris County residents migrated to Sussex County, especially the Hardyston-Vernon area.

In the early 1800s, people came to the area chiefly by way of the Paterson-Hamburg Turnpike, and after 1870, via the railroad. In the mid-1800s, the principal hamlet in the present four townships was Hamburg. Later, Franklin and Ogdensburg developed unique and intensive mining interests, prompting the desire for independence. In 1872, the New Jersey Midland Railroad put track in place through the area and proposed stations at Snufftown, Ogdensburg, Franklin, Hamburg, and Deckertown. The arrival of the railroads had a big impact on the area: city dwellers arrived for summer vacation, and city industries—creameries, manufacturers, and mills, and icehouses—relocated here to be near the railroads for transportation and among the lakes and forests for natural resources.

The people of the valley are also interrelated. Members of the Ogden family of Ogdensburg and the Haines family of Hamburg and the Fowler family of Franklin all intermarried. Inventor Thomas Edison became involved with local mining operations due in a fundamental way to his grandmother's being an Ogden. Many less prominent but no less valuable families of farmers intermarried and stayed in the area, resulting in long-lasting family groups and a stable population, which from 1800 to 1920, remained at about 23,000 residents.

I hope you enjoy this book. It is a tribute to the hardships and industry of our predecessors and the legacy they have left us.

—William R. Truran

One

HARDYSTON

Land of long mountains, summer lakes, and dairy farms.

In the mid-1700s, Sussex County was practically left off of maps. It was a frontier, a wilderness area in which pioneers settled. Indian attacks were feared. Legend tells of a fort built on Holland Mountain near the present Rock Oak Lodge in the early 1760s. The fort was manned by frontier guards. Some vestiges of its remains have been suggested. In the late 1760s, the focus shifted from fear of Indians and the French to discontent with the British and their Tory, or Loyalist, sympathizers. Col. John Seward, a patriot leader from Hardyston, was known as "the Terror of the Tories" for his exploits.

The close of the French and Indian War, *c.* 1760, and the growth of the colonies that were then British from early Dutch influence brought many new settlers into the area. As more people came in, they wanted to have their own local control and input to government. Hardyston Township was formed in 1762 and named after Josiah Hardy, who was New Jersey governor from 1761 to 1763.

Although not the earliest settlers, those who came and shaped Hardyston Township represent a lineage that starts in the mid-1700s and continues into the 1800s. The names include Rorick, Munson, Fowler, and Ames in Franklin Furnace; Wallings, Haines, and Lawrence in Hamburg; Ogden in Ogdensburg; and Seward, Ford, Strait, Margarum, Beardslee, and Cary in Hardyston, as it is known today. Over the years Hardyston was reduced in size as areas that had particular interests became town centers themselves.

Early settlers in east Hardyston worked with the iron ore present and used the waterpower of the Pequannock River for forges to produce iron. Men like John O. Ford developed Windham Forge and Stockholm Forge, and the Walthers family used the river for a tannery. David Strait was a wheelwright for settlers heading west in the mid-1800s. The Fords supplied land for the Methodist church.

In west Hardyston, farming and tending of cattle and sheep were performed by families like Beardslee, Scott, Monell, Simpson, Simmons, Edsall, and Rude. They took the wool to places such as Beardslee's Mill on White Pond Brook for fulling and the grain to the gristmills at Sharpsboro or near Greer's at Franklin Furnace.

Every hamlet in Hardyston Township had a tavern, which served as a gathering place to hear the latest news and to hold town meetings. Many of the taverns provided lodging as well. Travel was by carriage, stagecoach, horse, or foot. A distance of only 20 miles a day was not uncommon. Thus, lodging for wayfarers was available at many crossroads. The earliest known tavern in the area was on the northeast corner of the Route 23–94 crossroads. It was later replaced by a tavern and lodging in Smith's Hamburg Hotel. Francis Hamilton built lodgings close by on the Vernon Road, and Alexander Hamilton built the Height's House on the Paterson-Hamburg Turnpike at one of the highest points in the Hamburg Mountains, near a tollhouse above Silver Lake. This may be the place that men from east Hardyston went for powdered tobacco, or snuff, and from which the name Snufftown was derived. Since hard cider was a common drink, apple trees were located throughout the area.

Schools of a century or more ago were generally one-room buildings that served all grades. According to historian and county superintendent Ralph Decker, there were nine schools within the greater Hardyston Township c. 1902. Listed with their enrollment, which totaled 701 students, they were Hamburg, 150; Franklin, 291; Monroe, 28; Holland, 36; North Church, 32; Hardystonville, 44; Rudeville, 48; Willistine, 24; and Stockholm, 48. As demographics changed, most of these schools closed, and the students consolidated into larger buildings. Franklin's disparity influenced their decision to secede from Hardyston.

With the advent of the railroad, summer vacationers visited the several large hotels in Snufftown, a name the railroad quickly changed to Stockholm, after the local forge. The railroads carried to the cities the local dairy produce from the creameries and wood and ice harvested from the local forests and ponds.

Over the last 50 years, many vacationers who built homes at the lakes, such as Tamarack and Beaver, later became year-round residents. Today, Hardyston is encountering a building boom for single-family homes, and small shopping malls are being developed within the town centers, as well as along Route 94 to Vernon, at the Route 23–Holland Mountain Road intersection, and on Wheatsworth Road.

Over the sweep of history, hamlets began with small groups of pioneers with common interests, such as mining, forge operations, and milling. The hamlets within today's Hardyston Township (or shared with neighboring towns) include the following:

EAST HARDYSTON
Snufftown
Willistine
Windham and Canistear
Lakes: Beaver, Girard, Stockholm,
    Tamarack, Summit, and Deer Trail

WEST HARDYSTON
North Church
Big Springs
Harmonyvale
Hopkins Corner
Beaver Run
Monroe

NORTH HARDYSTON
Rudeville
Hardistonville
Scenic Lakes

This land of long mountains, summer lakes, and dairy farms is known as East Hardyston. Just inside the eastern edge of Sussex County was the Stockholm station, one of two station stops in the township. It was part of the New York, Susquehanna & Western Railroad line that came into Sussex County from the eastern approach, the line that succeeded the Midland Railroad. Although now gone, the station was one of the most modern and well-equipped of its day, with construction typical of the stations of the New York, Susquehanna & Western. At one time, large piles of cord wood lined both sides of the tracks as far as the eye could see, waiting to be shipped to metropolitan areas. Transportation to and from the station was supplied by Denton W. Clark in an open-air bus or, before 1910, in a horse-drawn carriage pulled by Molly, with an engineering unit of one horsepower.

AROUND THE BLOCK, STOCKHOLM, N.J.

Wouldn't you like to take a "spin" with G. T.

The Paterson-Hamburg Turnpike was the main street in the hamlet of Snufftown. This view was taken at the T, where the choice was to go left to Franklin Furnace or head straight over the mountain to Hamburg on the turnpike via the stagecoach road that was built *c.* 1804. Stone markers, placed every few miles, indicated it was "56 miles to Hoboken" or ". . . miles to Jersey City." One marker is now at the Hardyston Municipal Building. Three markers are still in existence on the old road. (Courtesy John Kolic.)

Along this area, the turnpike passed several commercial buildings. One of them was the Edsall Hotel, known *c.* 1860 as the Hotel I. Rude. Edsall was a very common name in the mid-1800s in Hardyston Township, with about 20 dwelling and properties owned by an Edsall.

The Hiram Utter Hotel was a large boardinghouse and hotel close to the train station.

The Kincaid Hotel stood across the T of the Snufftown and Vernon crossroads. It was known in the 1860s as the Snufftown Hotel. In the late 1800s, Snufftown, along with the rest of Sussex County, was a summer resort visited by city people who came by train. The Kinkaid was the most prestigious place in town. Beatrice Henderson's father worked there as a driver of horses and carriages and took boarders to places of interest and scenic importance. (Courtesy John Kolic.)

Winters in the late 1800s had plenty of snow, and the mode of transportation was horse and sleigh. In some ways, travel in the snow was smoother and easier than it was along rutted and muddy roads, in which carriages often got stuck. (Courtesy John Kolic.)

Sitting outside the Kinkaid Hotel, a vacationer with his pipe awaits a carriage while reading the paper. He will alight the carriage by means of the stone steps near the road. Note the strollers on the other side of the stagecoach road. Snufftown was a busy place. (Courtesy Helen and William Wurst.)

This general store was on the southeast corner of what is today known as Snufftown Road and Route 515. It was owned by James and Josephine Lewis. Lewis was the son of Seth Lewis, who came from Wales to Fishkill, New York, in the wholesale fur business. George (James's son) and Anna Lewis lived here also until the building burned down in March 1918, and then they opened the Lewis Hillside Villa.

At the tanbark mill, bark was ground to give color to leather. This tannery was on the upper part of the Pequannock River. Its power was furnished by a waterwheel. The mill was located across the Hamburg Paterson Turnpike from the Walther house. George Walther took over the tannery from Joseph Fleming and operated it until his death in 1887. (Courtesy Harvey Barlow.)

17

Arthur Walther and his sister Sarah lived here into the 1950s. They were the grandchildren of David Strait, a wheelwright who worked at Windham Forge. Strait's daughter Phoebe married George Walther who emigrated in 1825 from Wurtenburg, Germany, and became a well-known tanner. This has been known as the old Walther house, with the new one the present Rowett house, on the corner. (Courtesy Helen and William Wurst.)

David Strait was born in 1790 in Milton. Using many of the same tools as a carpenter, Strait hand-turned spokes and hubs from local oaks to create hundreds of wheels for the wagons that carried countless pioneers from this area to new homes in the West. According to Haines's history, people left this area c. the 1820s because of hard times here. Many from the Hardyston area settled in Ohio, around Columbus.

Among Hardyston's most famous people is Col. John Seward, "the Terror of the Tories." He settled here prior to 1767 and fought during the Revolutionary War. He was a freeholder, captain of the 2nd Regiment, Sussex Troops, and later colonel. He helped drive off bands of Tories (British Loyalists), who "infested" Snufftown Mountain. Seward's homestead burned down in the mid-1800s, and Noah Margarum built this house, which also burned and was replaced. Col. John Seward was the father of Dr. Samuel Swezy Seward of Florida, New York, and the grandfather of William Henry Seward, the U.S. secretary of state who acquired Alaska from Russia for about $7 million. Since the purchase was thought to be foolish at the time, it was called "Seward's Folly." (Courtesy Helen and William Wurst.)

This is Tory Rock. Story has it that on this site a Tory was hiding in wait as Col. John Seward was to pass by. The Tory was scared off before he had a chance to shoot Seward. The rock is north of the Seward house and is located in Vernon Township. It was reduced in size when Route 515 was widened some years ago. (Courtesy Helen and William Wurst.)

The Stockholm Schoolhouse, with its belfry and hand-rung bell, stood across from the Methodist church. Built c. 1888, this two-room grammar school at one time had 100 students. After the late-1890s Newark watershed project bought up much of the land, the Stockholm population dropped to the point that in the 1950s there were only about half that number of students. (Courtesy John Kolic.)

Here is a 1918 Republic school bus. The Stockholm bus had wooden seats and oilcloth curtains tacked to the windows to keep out the dust. The teacher is Helen Kinkaid, and the man in the far left window is Denton W. Clark. D. W. Clark supplied school transportation for many years. Although not shown here, the Rudeville school still stands and is a private residence today. (Courtesy D. W. Clark family.)

21

Only 14 years after the Revolutionary War, the Bethel Methodist Episcopal Society at Snufftown was begun. Wesleyan Methodism was associated with the Church of England—thus the name change. The congregation was likely visited by the famous traveling preacher Francis Asbury. The Sunday school was probably organized in 1815. Construction of the Stockholm Methodist Church was begun in June and completed by Christmas 1826. It was on the Hamburg circuit and is thought to be the oldest building in Stockholm. (Courtesy John Kolic.)

"LEWIS HILLSIDE VILLA," STOCKHOLM, N. J.

George and Anna Lewis opened the Lewis Hillside Villa after they moved from the Lewis General Store. The Hillside Villa was pieced together from other buildings. Known as Jorgensen's for many years, the restaurant recently became Victoria's. (Courtesy John Kolic.)

Brown's Store was one of the several businesses that kept rural folks stocked with dry goods and general merchandise. It was opened in April 1872 by William S. Longstreet, who came up the mountain from Franklin Furnace. Longstreet was also postmaster following Hiram Strait. Brown's was located near the Methodist church. The Dunn Store was near the church parsonage. (Courtesy Helen and William Wurst.)

LOG CABIN

The Willistine section of East Hardyston possessed a blacksmith shop, church, graveyard, and school. No longer in existence, the hamlet was located near the present middle of town, south of the First Aid Building. The Log Chapel at Willistine was built in 1866 by the residents of the neighborhood, with material supplied by Franklin Iron Company, Reverend Haines, and John Brown. The last service was performed in the chapel in 1903. The old graveyard, known as Wood's, Walker, or Willistine Cemetery, has Revolutionary War–period graves that can still be seen. Near the Passaic County border, the community of Windham developed. It used a pond and a vertical drop in the Pequannock River to power its industry. (Fred J. Stephens collection.)

The Windham Forge was located on the Pequannock River near the border of Sussex and Passaic Counties. It was built by John O. Ford c. 1790, after he left his holdings in Franklin Furnace. It was then operated by Sidney Ford, who lived in a large house nearby. Iron ore was plentiful in this part of Sussex County, and the old forges in Franklin Furnace, Sharpsboro, Sodom, and Sparta were among the first industries. To smelt the iron, charcoal fires had to be hot. To increase the heat, large bellows forced air onto the fire. The driving power to work the bellows was provided by waterwheels; thus, proximity to streams with good flow and vertical drop was essential. This was the last operating iron forge on the Pequannock River. Woodcutters supplied the wood for used in a smoldered fire to produce the charcoal that was burned in the furnace. Most of the countryside in the area was stripped bare for the wood for charcoal. Windham was named either after the town in Connecticut from which John O. Ford's great-grandfather came or after the "Wingdam" Forge, as David Strait spoke it, a word defined as "a dike that diverts a river." A road was constructed c. 1846 from Windham northeast to Canistear, a hamlet of Vernon, particularly for deliveries of ore to the Windham Forge.

Booth Brothers Knife Works was a well-known trademark. The father and son were immigrants from England and operated the plant for 15 to 20 years. The factory was located on the Pequannock River, which supplied waterpower. It stood about one-half mile south of the railroad station, just over the county border at the present intersection of Route 23 and Canistear Road. When the city of Newark purchased this property in 1903, the factory moved to Deckertown (Sussex) and the building burned down. Many of the 60 men who worked here followed the factory up to Sussex.

This view, taken on the way back to the Stockholm station, shows the creamery nearby. It was operated by John Einken and was typical of the commerce that developed near the railroads as they arrived c. 1870 and onward, taking local milk to the cities. The creamery is also long gone, with no remnant left. There were at least four creameries in Hardyston: in Stockholm, in Beaver Run, on the Sussex Railroad in Monroe at the Sparta border, and on the Lackawanna & Hudson River Railroad at Kimble's (or Ackerman) Crossing and known at various times as Fulboam's, R. F. Stevens, and Borden's.

The lakes region includes Beaver Lake, Lake Gerard, Lake Stockholm, Lake Tamarack, Summit, and Deer Trails. The lake communities of today began, in part, as a means of easing and speeding rail transportation. The railroads spawned the development of creameries, wood-cutting and ice-harvesting businesses, and tourism. Several of the lakes began as ice makers. From the Stockholm station, known at one time as Two Bridges, the trip to Beaver Lake was two miles. The station served an important function. Here, at this rare straight, wide, and flat area, there were sidings available for waiting trains. With steam-powered locomotives, the pull up Munson's Gap (Beaver Lake Mountain) was tough and required coal pockets and water stops about halfway up the mountain and sometimes at the top at Beaver Lake.

Post Office, Beaver Lake, N. J.

Just behind the Beaver Lake station is the old Beaver Lake post office. This rather venerable and primitive building served from 1906 to 1960, having been moved to the Clark's garage in the later years. The mail delivery was then moved to the Franklin post office. In earlier years, postmasters were political appointees. Thus, for example, the Kinkaid Hotel owner, a Democrat, and the Lewis Store owner, a Republican, across the street, traded the job every three years from 1883 to 1914—about nine times.

The Viaduct.   BEAVER LAKE, N. J.

A major obstacle for traveling by carriage or car was the steep road at Beaver Lake. Shown here is the bridge that existed early in the 1900s. This bridge was replaced when Route 23 widened the roadway in 1930 as a bridge next to it to span the two high points. The Beaver Lake train station and the post office were just below here. (Courtesy John Kolic.)

The earliest settler at Beaver Lake was peg-legged hermit William "Hype" Collins, who lived in a tiny log cabin on a small island with his dogs. Collins lived by hunting, trapping, and fishing. He rowed his boat in a reverse position so he "could see where he was going." Some campers followed in the 1890s, and in 1905, Beaver Lake was purchased by a group of people interested in having a summer cottage. This is the community center near the lake. (Courtesy John Kolic.)

Here is one of the beautiful views from a point named for the owner. Some of the men awoke before dawn, hiked to the Beaver Lake station, took the train to New York City for work, and returned at night—an unusually long commute in those days. Day hikes were made through wooded paths to other lakes, down to the Franklin Furnace general store for provisions, or perhaps to Beierle's in Ogdensburg for ice cream. Much camaraderie was evident within the Beaver Lake community, including vespers on the lake and boat parades with the Hamburgh National Band and other groups playing tunes such as "By the Light of the Silvery Moon." (Courtesy John Kolic.)

Lake Gerard, along with Summit Lake, was owned by the Brady Ice Company and was known as Brady's Pond. The ice was harvested in the winter months, stored in huge wooden sheds 60 by 120 feet long or longer, and packed with sawdust for insulation and separation. Lake Gerard had 14 icehouses and Summit Lake had 4 or 5. Some 100 men worked in the ice trade, with additional men working as teamsters and for the railroad. A total of about 30 rail cars of ice a day were shipped, mainly to Jersey City. A railroad siding at Stockholm, known as Summit Switch, allowed transport to the cities where the ice was used for ice cream and dairy purposes and for cooling and drinks at hotels. Many of the hotels in the area had adjoining icehouses. (Courtesy John Kolic.)

After Beaver Lake, Lake Stockholm was developed (c. 1926) by investors from Butler with Mrs. Cahill, in real estate. Don Amend built a number of homes, mainly in the Jefferson section. Later, Paul Negri developed some homes and then developed Lake Neepaulin. Lake Stockholm is partly in Jefferson Township. Lake Tamarack was developed next, acquired by hotel owner Edward Kinkaid from the Hudson Terminal Ice Company. Tamarack had a dam as early as 1870. Summit Lake was also purchased from an ice company by the Crane Company, builders of Lake Mohawk, in 1947, and Deer Trail Lakes were purchased in 1952 by Ken Henderson. Silver Lake is a YMCA camp. Scenic Lakes (part in Hardyston and also in Vernon) was developed in 1956. (Courtesy John Kolic.)

The Tamarack Corral is located outside of Lake Tamarack on Route 23. Over the years the place has been Cicere's and several other restaurants. In 1956, the Catholic mass was held here by Msgr. Stephen Dabkowski. In 1958, the St. John Vianney parish built a church nearby on land purchased from the Newark watershed project. (Courtesy John Kolic.)

Hardyston's prominent citizens

Seward Family

- John Seward entered the Second Regiment of Sussex Volunteers at the outbreak of the Revolution, later a Colonel
- Became famous in shooting an English spy in Snufftown
- An early resident, prior to 1767, on 46 acres in the Highlands of northern Snufftown, with a home constructed for strength and protection, known as the "double log house"
- Fought in the battles of Long Island and White Plains
- Said to have a friendship with George Washington, perhaps the General stayed with him some time on Snufftown Mountain
- Helped lead troops that manned the blockhouses along the Delaware River
- with 50 English pounds on his head, survived an incident at Tory Rock just north of home
- Grandson William H. Seward was Secretary of State in President Lincoln's Cabinet; "Seward's Folly" being the purchase of Alaska, one of the U.S.'s best decisions

Ford Family

- John O. Ford worked the Franklin Furnace until about 1790 and then built the Windham Forge east of Snufftown and near the border with Passaic County on the Pequannock River; also an early larger landowner
- John O. Ford also operated several other forges built sometime after 1800
- Charles and Rachel Ford deeded land for the Methodist Church in the year 1826
- Sidney Ford continued the operation of the Windham Forge for many years, making blooming iron and anchors

Lodging, tourism, and farming

Instrumental in the development of Hardyston were several families involved in lodging and later vacationers from the heat, fumes, and bustle of the cities. These included:

- **The Edsall Family**: one Edsall an owner of a hotel in Snufftown, and also family of farmers, about 15 locations noted in 1860, including an iron mine.
- **The Rude Family**: another extended family with a number of farms in the north central Hardyston, in Hardystonville and the appropriately named Rudeville area
- **Kincaid Family**: owned the popular Kincaid in Snufftown, postmaster, civic leaders.
- **Lewis Family**: similar to Kincaid, a family of merchants, storeowners, restaurant, automobiles
- **Clark**: Three generations of school transportation, charter members in Beaver Lake

Represented here are some of Hardyston's outstanding citizens.

"HIGH POINT SHADY REST"
Restaurant - Grill
Route 23   Beaver Lake, N. J.

A roadside establishment reminiscent of the roadhouses of the 1920s is the Shady Rest. It was known as "going to church" for some hardy Lake Gerard souls, who tipped a glass on Sunday mornings while vacationing in the woods of Hardyston. Beer could be purchased by walking up to the window. The Shady Rest burned down and is now an empty lot along Route 23 just east of the Beaver Lake bridge. (Courtesy John Kolic.)

One of the earliest buildings in the area was the Cary Meeting House, located in the present North Church Hardyston Cemetery. A later building affiliated with the Presbyterian Church of Sparta burned down in 1830, and a newer church was opened at the foot of the cemetery hill at the northeast corner of the road intersection. A parsonage was built in 1858 just to the east of the church, replacing one built in 1788. Services ended c. 1905, and the building was torn down in 1958, to be replaced by a municipal garage. (Courtesy Joan Bennetts Simmons.)

On the south side of North Church Road from Franklin was the wood frame building on the westerly tract of Beardslee's farm that served as the North Church school building. The road, which once came from the south, was redirected when the railroad was built in the early 1870s.

36

The Simmons Farm was located on Wheatsworth Road (Gingerbread Castle Road, in Hamburg). It was near the property where the new Hardyston Middle School was recently built. The picture bears the caption "Jacob Simmons and his wife Blanche Beemer Simmons, children George B., Katharyn, Roland, David on the farm of his father's." (A. J. Bloom photograph; courtesy Joan Bennetts Simmons.)

The Simpsons had their picture taken in front of their homestead, built c. 1820 between Hamburg and North Church. This was the site where George Washington's troops are believed to have encamped in 1778 and 1781 on travel between New York State and southern points. This farm hosted the 200th anniversary celebration of Hardyston Township on June 30, 1962.

The stone farmhouse at Big Springs, where this picture of the Seymour Day family was taken, was built in 1820 by Samuel Tuttle. Owned by J. Kimble in the 1860s, it is still a working farm.

The hamlets of Hardyston Township—Harmonyvale, Hopkin's Corner, and Beaver Run—have thrived in the past and today have a growing population. At one time or another, these hamlets had foundries, blacksmith shops, a creamery, a general store, a school, a post office, and many old farms on the beautiful rolling hills. Monroe, like these hamlets, is split between Hardyston and neighboring towns. Although most of Monroe is in Sparta Township, Hardyston hosted the schools of Monroe and several farms. Just to the south of the Big Springs farm is another stone house, built in 1822, with a farm that kept a breed of cattle found on only a very few U.S. farms. The cows were aptly named Dutch Belted cattle and came from Holland. There was much subtle Dutch influence in Sussex County despite the Dutch formal presence ending in 1664. The property was owned in the mid-1900s by Frank Dennis and more recently by the Conforths.

The Monroe Stone School House is located adjacent to the old Coyle farm. Kate Coyle taught at this one-room school. The school was constructed prior to 1819 of stone from a nearby quarry. The school was deeded to District No. 63 in 1892 and functioned until 1927. Today, the Stone School House is a museum and historic location.

Monroe area students went north a few hundred yards from the stone schoolhouse to the wood frame one on the hill c. 1926. This building has served for many recent years as a church.

Monroe was once known as Monroe Crossing. Crossing was a commonplace name in the early 1800s, denoting the settlement where two roads met and passed each other. A crossing was often a place for a store and for lodgings for weary travelers who made those few miles by stagecoach or horse. In Monroe Corners, there was the Monroe Inn, and opposite was the Sutton Store (later sold to Frank Smith). On the northwest corner was the Congleton Store and post office. Monroe was originally in Hardyston and later in Sparta, but always the center of the center of community activities.

The Bend Inn was a filling station and establishment on the way from Hamburg to Sussex on Route 23 north, which mainly followed the old Paterson-Hamburg Turnpike that turned into the Deckertown Pike, just before the old Ogden bridge—all of which originated c. 1804. The inn was later known as Castle Inn and Dale's. It was "the last Dale's in NJ" and also "where the music is on the house," with the notable piano up on the roof. Today, it is Winner's. This area of North Hardyston is the top part of what is also west and east and includes Scenic Lakes, new town houses, and golf course homes. These latter two developments originally were limestone quarries: Windsor (or Bodnar's and Crystal Springs) in Hardyston, and Ajax (or the Quarry and Heritage Lakes) in Hamburg. (Courtesy Harvey Barlow.)

Two

OGDENSBURG

Home of the Sterling Zinc Mine, tied with Edison's Iron Mine

Ogdensburg—or "the Burg," as it is commonly known—is 2.8 square miles and straddles Route 517, an early road south to Morris County. After arriving at the Hudson River in 1609, the Dutch began exploring the area for mineral resources. They found copper and iron ore in the Minisink Valley and along the Delaware River, and settled there. Further exploration brought discovery in the area later to be known as Ogdensburg. The English superceded the Dutch after 1664, and in 1761, the lands were claimed for Lord Stirling (William Alexander). Mining operations were named after him, although the name was altered over the years to Sterling Hill. As with the Dutch before them, however, the English were unable to effect useful product from the mine. In the meantime, iron ore was being gathered and refined in forges throughout the area.

The first known permanent settler in the area was Robert Ogden, who moved to Sussex County in 1778 from Elizabethtown (now known as Elizabeth). Ogden's family included several outstanding patriots who fought with George Washington. His move to the wilderness of remote Sussex County was due in large part to the British presence around Elizabethtown. Ogden acquired a large amount of land and built a frame house on the hill between Wilson Drive and the Ogdensburg-Sparta Road. It is said that in 1779, during George Washington's march from Newburg to Morristown, various advance segments of Washington's army camped on the Ogden farm in and around the schoolyard overlooking the Wallkill Valley. The Ogden house was torn down in the 1950s.

The Ogdens were a large family. While some sons went to war, some stayed and tended the land in Sussex County, which included apple and peach trees and a distillery that produced peach and apple brandy. Ogden himself was very active in the Presbyterian church. He first held services at his home and then established the first Presbyterian church in the area, at the headwaters of the Wallkill River in the Sparta section of Hardyston Township. Even after Ogden's death in 1787, family members kept active in the area, mining iron ore at their mine atop Sparta Mountain, and operating the forge on the Wallkill River.

Ogdensburg typified a mining town, with the Ogden Forge refining iron ore and the New Jersey Zinc Company mining zinc ore.

In 1820, farmer John Lanterman purchased land behind the present school site from the Ogden family. He burned lime and made bricks that were sold throughout Sussex County and also carted to New York by wagon. A man named McKiernan was another purchaser of a large tract of the Ogden estate.

In 1853, the post office was established and included a route to Newton. The Ogdensburg store was run by John George. The Ogden Mine Railroad, which opened in 1868, impacted Ogdensburg. The mule-powered wagon routes were changed from the path through Sparta over Signal Hill and then Morris County, to a haul road up the mountain to the new railroad. This transportation route probably solidified Thomas Alva Edison's decision some 15 years later to invest millions of dollars in the iron mine and briquette operation. The Midland Railroad ran down Beaver Lake Mountain and through Ogdensburg, switching back to Franklin Furnace, with a spur connecting the Sterling Mine to the railroad. The building of this road was prompted by the mining companies at Sterling Hill to facilitate transport of zinc ore to smelting plants. Later, an upper track also descended from Beaver Lake Junction through Sparta and out to points west.

About the same time as the rail line came to town, Nobadiah Wade built the Ogdensburg House. Also, local newspapers heralded the opening of the Adam House as a new hotel and restaurant. This later became Sweney's and the Lyon House. The Edison mining operations had built and housed some 1,000 people in the new town of Summerville by c. 1890. Thomas Edison frequently stayed in town, usually at the Lyon House.

In the late 1890s and early in the 1900s, the town's streets were laid out and John Lanterman built a store, which was later owned by Patrick Madden, who added an opera house that was also used for town meetings. Also in the town were a movie theater over Dolan's Garage, Dolan's Ogdensburg Hotel, John Sweney's Lyon House, Huss's south end bakery and butcher shop, and Thomas Lawrence's and Mr. Chambers's lumber company, started in 1875 near the train station.

Employment remained mainly in mining, at Bigelow and Swain Limestone (later Farber and Cemex, and closed in 2003) and at the large and successful Sterling Hill operation, which was consolidated c. 1900 into the New Jersey Zinc Company and lasted until 1986, when the Sterling Hill Mine, the last operating mine in New Jersey, closed.

Today, Ogdensburg is a quiet bedroom community, with some new housing developments near the edge of town. The hamlets in Ogdensburg and vicinity include the following:

Ogdensburg
Main Street
Sterling Hill
Sodom
Summerville
Cuckoo Flats

This scene shows the train from Beaver Lake arriving at Ogdensburg. St. Thomas Aquinas Roman Catholic Church is on the right, along with Railroad (now Kennedy) Avenue. A lumberyard also stood near the station. (Courtesy Harvey Barlow.)

St. Thomas Aquinas Roman Catholic Church was built in 1881. It burned and was rebuilt in 1912. The church also has a rectory. (Courtesy Ogdensburg Historical Society.)

This is the Presbyterian church in Ogdensburg. In 1879, John George, superintendent of the Sterling Mine, gave land for the church. The building was dedicated on December 15, 1880. (Courtesy John Kolic.)

This eastward view shows Railroad Avenue. The road was named Railroad Avenue after the railway was built through the town in the early 1870s. It was renamed Kennedy Avenue in the 1960s in honor of Pres. John F. Kennedy. On the left is the Baptist church. Three of the Burg's four churches are located on this avenue. The Ogdensburg Hotel is seen on the right. (Courtesy Sterling Hill Mine Museum.)

This view looks westward down Railroad Avenue near Main Street. The Presbyterian church is on the right. Joseph Lipsky, who owned a clothing store on Main Street, lived in the house on the left. (Courtesy Sterling Hill Mine Museum.)

North of the area where the firehouse now stands, the railroad to Franklin came down the great incline of Beaver Lake Mountain and passed over Main Street on the trestle shown here. The overpass was built in the 1870s. When the service was discontinued, the sandy soil was removed from the track bed, along with the trestle. One concrete pier remains farther west near North Clark Street. (Courtesy Ogdensburg Historical Society.)

This view was taken looking south from Beardslee's Hill toward Main Street. Owned by a Beardslee, one of the oldest homes in Ogdensburg is located on the right. Note the two-horse wagon on the way to Franklin Furnace. The route from the Franklin mines to Woodport on Lake Hopatcong through Sparta was a well-worn one. Cork Hill Road may also have been used. Beardslee's Hill is not to be confused with Beardslee's Mill. The latter was located in the Plains Settlement, in Franklin, and is where Samuel Fowler experimented with zinc oxide paint. (Courtesy Sterling Hill Mine Museum.)

With his horse kicking up dust, a man drives his buggy at a good clip along a dirt roadway in the northern end of Ogdensburg toward Franklin. A mansard-roofed home out of frame to the left was built by John George, who was Sterling Hill Mine superintendent from 1853 to 1880. (Courtesy Ogdensburg Historical Society.)

Here is a northward view of Main Street in Ogdensburg. The train trestle and road north to Franklin are in the distance.

This early-1900s view of Ogdensburg appears to be a print from a glass negative. Note the old dirt roads prevalent in all of the rural towns of northern Jersey. Hitching posts, for the horses, run the whole easterly side of the street. In the left foreground is the Ogdensburg Cash Store, which offered dry goods and groceries. Also on the left is the Madden store and opera house. (Likely an A. J. Bloom photograph; courtesy Sterling Hill Mine Museum.)

The Ogdensburg Cash Store is shown being repaired. Note the "kids being kids," some of them barefoot, while their elders peruse the latest news in the paper. (Courtesy Sterling Hill Mine Museum.)

The next building to the south of the Ogdensburg Cash Store contained the post office of John P. Madden. He enlarged the building and added an opera house.

MAIN ST., Ogdensburg, N. J.

Looking northeastward, this view shows Main Street in the 1920s. The storefronts have changed; automobiles are present; sidewalks have been installed; the hitching posts are gone. Note the street post sign that says, "Go Right." This must have been an accident-prone intersection with Railroad Avenue.

Main Street, Ogdensburg, N. J.

This view looks southward from the town center and includes the Ogdensburg Hotel. To the left behind the trees is Sweney's, also known as the Lyon House.

The Ogdensburg Hotel is shown in a view from the early 1900s. The hotel was owned by Patrick Dolan, and John Sweney operated it. To the left of the hotel is Dolan's store.

This view looks northward toward Sweney's and the main row of buildings in town. (Courtesy John Kolic.)

Here is one of two views of Sweney's. On this wintry but warm day, the local men have arrived from working in the mines. (Courtesy Sterling Hill Mine Museum.)

The second view is from the same time period but in a different season. Notice the hitching post for the horses, the raised platform for ease of entry into the carriage, and the planks to minimize problems with mud. The hotel and restaurant was built as the Adam House in 1873. It was then the Lyon House, and then John Sweney left Dolan's Ogdensburg Hotel and came across the street. (Courtesy Sterling Hill Mine Museum.)

Shown is the arrival of an important man, with his derby on and the schoolyard full of students dressed well and awaiting the visit. All of the town's schools were on this site. The first was a log cabin, present in 1804 and replaced in 1834 and again in 1856. In 1872, a two-story brick schoolhouse was built, partially demolished, and moved to be a firehouse, now the Ogdensburg Museum. (Courtesy John Kolic.)

Brick Building built 1821, Ogdensburg, N. J.

This view was taken just beyond the school on the way southeastward toward Sparta, Lake Hopatcong, and Morris County, where a number of the early settlers hailed from. This was the favored route since it had the least incline, an important factor in the age of horse-drawn carts and wagons. The house on the left, built in 1821, was recently torn down. (Courtesy John Kolic.)

This c. 1910 view of the Ogdensburg school shows the new addition, which was necessary because of the growing zinc-mining population (for both the Sterling Mine as well as the mine in Franklin—both owned by the New Jersey Zinc Company). The two-story brick addition added two classrooms and is considered the fifth school change. The school was torn down in 1930 to make way for the new one (shown below), but this addition was moved about 150 feet toward Passaic Avenue and was used as a firehouse until 1988, when a new firehouse was built near the old trestle location. This building, with state grants, became the home of the Ogdensburg Historical Society and Firehouse Museum.

This is the sixth school change. Built in 1927–1928, the brick structure had 12 classrooms, an auditorium, and rooms for the nurse, the office, and teachers. Note the deadman at the T in the road; similar ones were at Railroad Avenue and other locations in Ogdensburg and Franklin.

Hector Andrina   Howard Fatzinger   Paul Chomey

Shown is Ogdensburg's police force *c.* 1940. (Courtesy Ogdensburg Historical Society.)

Beyond the Main Street area of Ogdensburg is what is known today as Edison Road, heading up the mountain to the Ogden and Edison mines. Just west of the New York, Susquehanna & Western tracks of today was a blacksmith and wheelwright shop, shown here. George Tice is on the right, and his assistant, Lew "Peg" Willis, is on the left.

The men who were standing outside the blacksmith shop have been kind enough to move inside. In this 1905 photograph, George Tice is in the background, and Lew "Peg" Willis is manning the anvil and iron. Although it seems to be a remote location outside of town, the shop probably had many opportunities to shoe horses for the steep and long incline up to the mines. (Courtesy Sterling Hill Mine Museum.)

Mountain View, Ogdensburg, N. J.

The view from atop the mountain shows the laying of the right of way for the Midland Railroad, which came down from Beaver Lake Mountain and then swung north to Franklin Furnace. On the right, note the two trestles. Also note the spur to Sterling Hill, laid in 1872. The zinc mill can be seen in the middle left background. The Burg's Methodist church can be seen in the middle left of the photograph.

This bird's-eye view shows the still primitive operations at Sterling Hill, but it also shows a well-developed community of churches, commercial buildings, a school, a railroad station, and private homes. (Courtesy Sterling Hill Mine Museum.)

Here is a view of an Ogdensburg parade in the 1920s. (Courtesy Ogdensburg Historical Society.)

ROCK CUT, EDISON ROAD, OGDENSBURG, N. J.

This view looks back to the rock cut that is near the top of the mountain. From here, the trip to the world-famous Ogden and Edison mines is only a short distance. This way had been used for hauling the iron ore down to the Ogden Forge in Sodom before Edison arrived. The Ogden Mine Railroad was opened in 1868 (the year this roadway was cut) from Morris County and allowed the iron ore to be easily transported to Lake Hopatcong, where it could be carried by barge along the Morris Canal to smelting plants. The iron mines at Franklin Furnace then brought the ore by oxcart up the mountain to the railroad, thus greatly shortening the haul to Lake Hopatcong by the same oxcart by way of Sparta and over Signal Hill to Woodport. The haul up this hill lasted only for the few years until the railroad came to Franklin in 1872.

At the top of the mountain above Ogdensburg is Sparta Township, the home of the Ogden Mines. At the time shown, however, this is the town of Summerville and home of Thomas Edison's iron mining and refining operations. Although in Sparta Township, the Edison operations were chiefly considered to be related to Ogdensburg. (Courtesy Edison National Historic Site Archives.)

59

This view of Edison's operations shows that many of the new homes to be built in New City are not yet finished, although the lumber is there for them. Cuckoo Flats is in the foreground, and the building in the left foreground has the name conspicuously written across the front. To the right, out of the picture, is Summerville, and beyond that is Mudwall Row. The village was completely torn down, and many of the homes were taken to Ogdensburg, Franklin, Stockholm, and Milton. These homes are still in use today throughout the area. (Courtesy Edison National Historic Site Archives.)

From long ago, the area on the way up the hill on Passaic Street to town had dwellings on it. This home was occupied by Sybil Vaughan Devore, who stands with her a large milk container by the side of the house. This is probably an early picture because the rail line that heads up the mountain does not appear to be present. (Courtesy Sterling Hill Mine Museum.)

Ogdensburg's prominent citizens

Ogden Family

- Robert Ogden II (1716-1787), patriot, one of the town's earliest settlers, from Elizabethtown, about 1778
- Member of King's provincial council of NJ, member of Assembly and speaker of legislature, delegate Continental Congress 1775
- Started the first Presbyterian church in the Wallkill Valley.
- Son Lt.Col. Matthias and brother Aaron fought in many Revolutionary War battles, aided George Washington, rode under Lafayette
- Sons Robert Jr. and Elias tended local orchards, distillery, forge, and mines
- Phebe Hatfield Ogden(d 1796), wife of Robert II, named the town of Sparta, mother of 22 children, many of whom were great citizens in their own right

(Photos of the paintings of the Ogdens that are located at the Elizabeth museum, home of Governor Aaron Ogden provided by William and Mary Eleanor Eppler)

Thomas Edison

- One of America's greatest inventors adopted by Ogdensburg for his local impact
- Developer of the mine complex on top of Ogden Mountain
- Created village of Summerville atop the mountain with lights and running water for the residents.
- Wallkill Valley is still dotted with homes originally from Summerville and removed to the valley in the late 1800s

Patrick J. Dolan (1869-1927)

- Ogdensburg's first mayor
- Prominent in business, banking, education, and politics
- Worked from age 13 as clerk in a store owned by Patrick Madden
- Partner in the firm McCarthy and Dolan
- Freeholder, Tax Collector of Sparta, on Board of Ed
- Was 1st president of Sussex County Trust Company

Shown are some of Ogdensburg's prominent citizens.

MAIN ST. OGDENSBURG, N.J.

This view shows the middle of the town of Ogdensburg. Note that this is a different time period: no longer c. 1910 but in the 1940s. (Courtesy John Kolic.)

Ogdensburg in the 1940s had changed: paved roads, newer cars, no horses or hitching posts, and the trees have grown to a large size. (Courtesy John Kolic.)

N. J. ZINC CO. R. R. BRIDGE, Ogdensburg, N. J.

Shown is the bridge at Sterling Hill. This railroad trestle was originally at Mine Hill in Franklin and can be seen in one of the pictures under Franklin *c.* 1900. It once spanned the Wallkill River from the area near the Franklin Pond Falls. The bridge to the Sterling Mine is still in place, although the track servicing the site has been removed. (Courtesy John Kolic.)

WALLKILL ARCH BRIDGE, OGDENSBURG, N. J.

Here is a twin arch bridge. The stone arches spanned the Wallkill River as it passed northeast of the Sterling Hill Mine. This installation was described widely as "the backward tunnel," as the original intent was for the roadway tunnel to be larger than the river tunnel. It did not turn out that way. Some newspapers at the time of construction (1871) indicate that the tunnel was built correctly. (Courtesy John Kolic.)

63

This is a view of the Sterling Mine and Mill from Bridge Street. The photograph was taken by Joe Stefkovich in 1917 while he was surveying for the new company homes to be put in this area. Other home were built on Avenue A, Avenue B, Bridge Street, and Plant Street, where many of the miners and their families who came from eastern Europe and the Southwest lived. These homes were similar to the bungalows in Franklin on Sterling Street. Other New Jersey Zinc Company homes were built on top of Sterling Hill. Those on Arch Street were known as the Better Homes in Franklin. (Courtesy Michael Stefkovich.)

This is a view of the Sterling Mine and Mill from Bridge Street. The photograph is from the NJZC surveyor records. It was taken when the new company homes were being built. Other NJZC homes were built on Avenue A, Avenue B, Bridge Street, and Plant Street, where many of the miners and their families who came from eastern Europe and the American Southwest lived. These homes were similar to the bungalows in Franklin on Sterling Street. Other NJZC homes were built on top of Sterling Hill. Those on Arch Street were the same as those known as the Better Homes in Franklin. (Courtesy Michael Stefkovich.)

In the stories and history of the area, one section was typified as a sinful place where people consumed "cheap whiskey and the concoction of deviltry." The place was called Sodom by Ogdensburg residents in the early 1900s and was so named on boundary descriptions when the town seceded from Sparta. Shown is the area spoken of, mainly at the foot of Railroad (now Kennedy) Avenue near the Wallkill River. The Ogdensburg Ogden Forge was at the far right, and the area of it that was worked was at the bottom of the hill below where the railroad station later stood. The horses took the ore up the steep hill, or "thank you m'am" because there was a place to rest at the top, and then they took the ore onto the charging bridge over to the forge where it was dumped in. (Courtesy Sterling Hill Mine Museum.)

This depiction shows how the Ogdensburg Ogden Forge may have looked. It is a rendering of the Andover Forge. Compare this with the Windham Forge photograph in the Hardyston section. The water powered the bellows that added air to the fire to increase the temperature within the hearth. It also ran the hammer that worked off a trip mechanism. A forge was a very noisy, smoky, hot area. (Courtesy Helen and William Wurst.)

66

Three

FRANKLIN

The Fluorescent Mineral Capital of the World
and America's Model Mining Town.

Franklin may be a small local town, but it has world recognition. In any geologists' circle, Franklin is known for the rare minerals found only here and in Ogdensburg.

As with Hardyston, Hamburg, and Ogdensburg, the early town of Franklin centered around the forge. The town's history includes not only zinc ore but also iron ore. First known as Franklin Furnace, it had the most durable iron industry in Sussex County. A furnace was built c. 1770 along the Wallkill River not far from the site of the old Catholic church. Another forge is said to have been located north of town on the Wallkill River at White Bridge, near Fountain farm. The forges were fed bog iron, iron ore from just below or near the earth's surface, usually found in wet areas. Bog iron was also mined in the area near Maple Road known Ball's Hill.

The town was likely named for William Franklin (who was well known early in the 1770s), the colonial governor at the time, rather than for Benjamin Franklin. As early as 1765, William Potts is believed to have built the furnace at Franklin Pond, northwest of where the falls are now. He was sympathetic to England, as was William Franklin. A blast furnace was built in the early 1870s and was touted to be among the biggest in the nation. This furnace, and the iron age in Franklin, lasted until c. 1900. Afterward, the works and many of the tenement buildings on both sides of the pond and along Cork Hill Road were torn down.

Most notably mentioned for Franklin are the zinc deposits. As early as 1750, the outcrops on Mine Hill were deeded from the proprietors to the heirs of Anthony Sharpe of Sharpesboro, or Hamburg, who were working the iron forges but must have found to their dismay that the ore was nearly impossible to smelt. The land was conveyed to Samuel Fowler, Franklin's most prominent citizen. Fowler managed to find the means to produce marketable zinc, created new uses in the form of white paint, and sold the recognition of Franklin to the world before his death in 1844. Although a number of mines and mining corporations and litigation were all involved, the matter was resolved in the Great Consolidation of 1898, and from then on, the New Jersey Zinc Company produced over 22 million tons of zinc ore valued at over $500 million.

Without a doubt, Franklin was good for the New Jersey Zinc Company and without a doubt, the New Jersey Zinc Company was good for Franklin. The company created many jobs for new immigrants, even during the depths of the Great Depression, and cared for the families, offering them a company store, a hospital, a community club called the Nabe, housing, a fire department, water, telephone, electric power—all of the needs of the community.

Franklin was enriched by the many immigrant groups who came through: Irish in the mid-1800s, eastern Europeans (including many Hungarians) from the 1890s through 1910, the Cornish tin miners from 1905 to 1915, and Mexicans and Chileans from c. 1915 to 1920. Many merchants followed the miners to serve their needs.

The town was a rough-and-tumble place, and law and order was brought in by Police Chief Herbert Irons, a man with many stories to his name.

Franklin Furnace became Franklin Borough in March 1913. It remained exceedingly busy with the mining operations until 1954. Franklin was served by the New York, Susquehanna & Western, Lehigh & Hudson River, Sussex, Mine Hill, and Lackawanna and Western Railroads. In 1914, the town had a theater that was touted as "the best between New York City and Pittsburgh." Franklin's vocational-technical school was one of the best, having been modeled on the outstanding Gary, Indiana, system that advocated vocational training and departmentalization of the grades. Later, when this one building held kindergarten through grade 12, it was the only of its kind one in New Jersey until 1982. Focusing on its illustrious past, Franklin today is transforming itself by accentuating its local natural resources and heritage of hardworking immigrants.

Notably, the zinc mines and great variety of fluorescent ores have prompted the U.S. Congress to decree Franklin as "the fluorescent mineral capital of the world." The Wildcat Rock Shelter is now New Jersey Department of Environmental Protection land, where the archeological treasure honors cliff dwellers of 10,000 years ago. The hospital building, first in the county and built by the New Jersey Zinc Company, has been named as historically significant. Hamlets within the borough of Franklin include the following:

Franklin Furnace
Mine Hill
South Franklin
Munsonhurst
The Junction
Greenspot
Old Main
High Street
Plains Settlement
Mexico
Siberia
Better Homes

Two railroads, the Lackawanna and the Susquehanna, used the same station, which was known as Franklin's Union Station. Art Holly is the driver of the horse and wagon in this and other images. Aaron Holly of Hamburg died in the 1950s. His son Jim Holly ran the auto taxi service.

This c. 1860–1867 photograph shows Franklin Furnace under way with waterpower and charcoal. The Wallkill River is seen in the foreground, and robust operations are evident. There are several buildings, most importantly (but not prominently) is the furnace, to the right center. It is thought that the first full white building at the right center was a general store of Oakes Ames, and the white one behind it was superintendent William Ames's in-town residence. The famous Massachusetts Ames family owned many homes and mining interests in Franklin at the time. This operation lasted until almost 1900 and worked the iron ore deposits that had been found mainly on Ball's or Doland's Hill, just behind and to the right. A number of prospects had been claimed and worked on the hill. Behind it is another hill. The Irish immigrants were among the major workers here in the 1860s, and they were mainly Catholic. A church was located behind the furnace, just out of sight. The cemetery for the church was located on top of Cork Hill, reputedly named for county Cork in Ireland. (Courtesy Franklin Mineral Museum.)

Shown is the Boston Franklinite Iron Company works. The railway came to this northwestern New Jersey area shortly after 1870 and, with it, easy delivery of anthracite coal from Pennsylvania, making large-scale smelting of iron from local ore possible here. Both the necessary iron and limestone for flux were found literally a few feet from the furnace. The works were so large that they were reputed to be among the largest in the nation in the mid-1870s. Good times were cyclical, however. By the beginning of the 20th century, the mining operation for iron was over and the works were completely dismantled and taken to Pennsylvania coal fields. (Courtesy Franklin Mineral Museum.)

This northeastward view of Buckwheat Hill (Mine Hill) in Franklin was taken c. 1908 from the train tracks just east of the Franklin Union Station. The intersection in the foreground is near today's First Aid Squad Building. To the right is the Franklin Quarry for limestone (now a pistol range), and in the upper left is what was the Taylor Mine (the Open Cut). The wooden tower was 150 feet high and was paired with the one to the left to haul ore and tailings out of the Open Cut. Barely visible in the center is a railroad bridge that spanned the Wallkill River below the falls and over to the lower edge of the Taylor Mine tailings dump. This bridge is still in existence, but at the mine at Ogdensburg over the Sterling Hill Road.

Road Scene, Franklin Lake, N. J. *You dont know what you will miss if you dont come soon.* Handcolored.

Taken from the Franklin Pond, this view looks eastward toward where later the A & P was for years, Stephens Corner Sunoco, and now the Mobil gas station. This area was known by some as South Franklin. (Courtesy John Kolic.)

View Around the Lake, Franklin, N. J.

This eastward view shows South Franklin, where a horse-drawn wagon or stage moves southward toward Munsonhurst. In the foreground a large area of Franklin Pond has been filled in with tailings from the mining operation. In the dim distance are two ore cars at the Sussex Limestone Company, another limestone quarry, which is still visible today behind the plaza across from the Franklin Diner. The company was served by a railroad spur of the New York, Susquehanna & Western line from Corkhill Road, through hill country, across the present-day Route 23 and Hardyston school area. The spur operated from c. 1900 to 1910. (Courtesy Harvey Barlow.)

71

This view looks southward toward Munsonhurst. Just to the right was at one time a grocery and later Durachko's Bar, some bottles from which were recently found in Franklin Pond's mud. The road ahead was used throughout much of the middle of the 1800s to transport ore from the Franklin mines by oxcart down through Ogdensburg and Sparta to Woodport on Lake Hopatcong, where the ore was taken by barge on the Morris Canal (begun c. 1824). This means of transportation was so expensive that it was compared with the cost of shipping ore from Europe. On the return the carts would haul coal. Later, c. 1864, a railroad went to the Ogden mines and then the ore was taken up what later was called Edison Road to the top for shipping to Rockaway. This route ceased c. 1870, when the Sussex Railroad came through Franklin, and then in 1872, when the New Jersey Midland (later the New York, Susquehanna & Western) Sussex Branch made it possible to reach Hoboken and the Midlands.

VIEW OF SOUTH FRANKLIN, N. J.

This is the road to Munsonhurst. To the far right is the Munson store that served the hamlet. (Courtesy John Kolic.)

72

On the road to Munsonhurst is Munson's Row, houses that are still standing and that were part of the community that included a distillery, sawmill, general store, farm, lime kiln, lodging, and horse team barns. To the left can be seen coal pockets for the community from the rail spur servicing the quarry, which was later known as Munson's Quarry. (Courtesy Harvey Barlow.)

Linking East Hardyston's Beaver Lake and Lake Gerard is the Black Brook, which winds down Beaver Lake Mountain through Munson's Gap. Black Brook's Gap also served as the route for the old road, the new Route 23, the rail track for the New York, Susquehanna & Western from Sparta, and the rail line from Ogdensburg.

73

The Munson family lived here in the 1700s. Israel Munson was born in Morris City in 1771. The location was a strategic intersection of commerce to the north and south, as well as the easterly approach to the Wallkill Valley through Munson's Gap from Beaver Lake Mountain. Samuel Munson is one of Franklin's outstanding citizens.

This view across Franklin Pond to the south has the Fowler Quarry (far right) at the edge of the iron mines and the original Catholic church (in the distance).

This photograph of the Franklin Pond Falls is timeless. Today, the view from the same spot is identical in the foreground. The background, however, no longer has the gristmill or the storehouses for the iron operations that were run here. The opening just below and to the right of the dam was the exit for the flume tunnel that fed the water to power the gristmill. (A. J. Bloom photograph.)

The Falls, Franklin Furnace, N. J.

This eastward view shows Franklin Falls. Note the boathouse on the left bank, which is said to have been used by New Jersey Zinc Company doctor Charles Dunning. Beyond is some of the housing, likely put up by the Boston Iron Company, for immigrant families, a number of which were Irish. This row house was labeled by R. M. Catlin as Cob Row, as in the male swans, since it was only single men who lived there. It burned down or was taken down c. 1908.

Swimming at the Franklin Pond was a highlight of the summer for the youth of the community. The New Jersey Zinc Company supported the people of Franklin with many of life's comforts: water, electricity, telephone, and hospital. The company also provided facilities at the pond, including a bathhouse, diving platforms, rafts, and guardhouses.

As on many other lakes in the area, ice was harvested on Franklin Pond. Men cut the ice and then hauled it to this conveyor, which moved it to the icehouse just west of the pond, close to the railroad tracks. (Sydney Hall collection.)

Pictured in the 1890s, Old Cork Hill Catholic Church was located south of Franklin Pond. In 1902, a new Catholic church was built near Col. Sam Fowler's. In the 1970s, the old church was owned by the Morgan family. The church building is no longer in existence. (Fred J. Stephens collection.)

The Fowler Quarry was located along Cork Hill Road, just south of Franklin Pond, across from the old Catholic church. It supplied lime that was used extensively as flux for iron making, both right at Franklin Furnace and elsewhere. A lime kiln still exists along these tracks near the Kovach Grove water spring. Another quarry, Bigelow & Swain Limestone, became Farber and then Cemex and then closed in 2003.

One of the town's most noted citizens was Herbert Irons. He came to Franklin when it was considered a rough-and-tumble mining town and, as police chief, worked hard to establish law and order. He helped make Franklin the model mining town it became. The first jail was located by Franklin Pond. Before it opened, criminals were taken to Newton, sometimes over the saddle on horseback. The police station was later established near the Palmer Shaft, along with the fire department (today's County Library). Then, in the 1990s, it was moved back down to the pond area. (Courtesy Franklin Mineral Museum.)

The Washington Hotel, located just below the train station, was a boardinghouse for single immigrant miners. The 1905 register book lists David W. McCarthy as the proprietor. (Courtesy Harvey Barlow.)

Shown is the bridge at the Franklin House. To the left are the barns, with the Wallkill River beyond. Several horse-drawn wagons traverse Church Street, heading toward the ironworks, barely seen in the distance. Several passenger cars are at Franklin's Union Station, on the hill in the center. The wood frame building to the right of the bridge is the old blacksmith shop. A gristmill was just to the right, out of the picture, until the rail bed was built c. 1870. Several of the buildings seen here were built and owned by the Ames family of Boston. Congressman Oakes Ames was asked in 1865 by Abraham Lincoln to build the Union Pacific Railroad. Lincoln said, "By building the Union Pacific you will become the remembered man of your generation." Ames did build the railroad but was involved in a scandal that compromised his success. (Courtesy Franklin Mineral Museum.)

The white barn on the far right is the wagon barn, part of the Franklin House complex. This picture, taken when Watson Littell owned the property, shows a wagon picking up goods at the bottling works. (Sen. Robert Littell collection.)

The Franklin House was the oldest hotel in town. It was owned by George W. Greer in 1860 or earlier. After Greer did away with drinking, it became known as the Temperance House, until Watson Littell purchased the property. Littell came up from Rockaway, where he was in the hotel business. He had a stable in the barn across the street in which a Mr. Fasolo worked renting buggies. Part of the building across the street was the company store for Thomas Edison's NJ & PCW mine above Ogdensburg, which Littell used for his bottling works. To the rear left is the old school, and to the rear right is the old Baptist church.

Watson Littell and some fellow passengers get ready for a buggy ride outside of the Franklin House. The Mine Hill can be seen in the distance. (Sen. Robert Littell collection.)

Just up the hill from the Franklin House, on Church Street, was the Crane General Store. Franklin had several general stores during the time when most people had no transportation other than by foot. Old photographs frequently showed a number of people walking the streets. The policeman in this photograph is likely Constable Finnigan, who held the post before the arrival of Chief Irons. Crane's also one of the many boardinghouses in town. As mining operations expanded, the town took in more boarders. With the difficulty in finding housing, immigrants without families used the "hot bed" method: when they went onto one of the three shifts at the mine, others coming off a shift would take their place in the bed. (Courtesy John Kolic.)

To the right is the 1824 church, first used as a Baptist church and then as a Presbyterian church and now as a Jewish synagogue. Among rock outcroppings here is the Sliding Rock, used by generations of schoolchildren to have fun and to create a sewing project for their mothers. A cannon reputedly made by Oakes Ames (or brought back from the Civil War) was mounted in a depression on a rock here. It was borrowed by Newton for its parade in 1895 and was never returned.

PUBLIC SCHOOL, Franklin, N. J.

Just behind the Crane General Store was the first Franklin School, on Oak Street. Earliest mention of a school in town was related to Amos Munson, born in 1803, who was to be educated by the "local district school." In 1892, the district celebrated the 400th anniversary of Christopher Columbus's arrival. In 1904, four rooms were added to the two existing rooms. This school was in operation when another school opened on top of the Mine Hill in 1915 as the vocational school (later the grammar and high school).

Here is the second-grade class of the Franklin Furnace grammar school in 1906. From left to right are the following: (first row) Harry Southard, Miles Condon, John Toth, Leslie Stephens, Russell Katzenstein, Clarence "Pat" Bailey, Bill Edwards, Arthur McCloud, and George Holley; (second row) unidentified, George Shauger, Carl Katzenstein, Chale Banta, Fred J. Stephens, Clinton Down, Roscoe McIntee, Henry Tidaback, Alfred Romyns, Fred Garrity, and Frank Hollis; (third row) teacher Blanch Beemer, ? Finnigan, Ruth Stanaback, Tillie Van Tassel, Janie Goll, Fred Shauger, and Joe Brooks. Next to the Oak Street school was the church in which the Baptists started out in 1823, the Presbyterians followed, and the Jews now have their synagogue. In the window on the door is a reflection of the mine superintendent's large house atop the hill. (Fred J. Stephens collection.)

Dr. Charles Dunning, the New Jersey Zinc Company physician, makes his rounds by horse and carriage in 1902. Dunning died in 1927 as a result of injuries sustained in a fall from the hayloft of the barn in which his two carriage horses were kept. The new company doctor was a young Canadian, Frederick John "Jack" Scott. He used Dunning's office, which was connected to the Dunning family home, on Oak Street. Margaret Dunning, the eldest daughter, was at first unhappy with this arrangement. However, in time, she and Scott became good friends and were married in 1933. Scott worked in the mornings at the company dispensary, a wooden building just to the left of the present library. He also saw patients at the Franklin Hospital and in the afternoons and evenings at his home office. In addition, he made house calls whenever he was needed—at all hours. When asked how many babies he had delivered, Scott always said, "More than half of the town." The actual number was somewhere between 2,000 and 3,000 babies, for the whopping charge of $25 each.

Dr. Samuel Fowler, the man who produced marketable zinc and created new uses in the form of white paint, is arguably Franklin's most important citizen. Dr. Fowler's mansion, on Stone Mill Road to the west of town, was destroyed by fire in the mid-1800s. His son was Col. Samuel Fowler (1818–1865), who commanded the 15th New Jersey Regiment, including Company D from Lafayette, Company I from Newton, and Company K from Hardyston. He also served, albeit only a few days, in the state legislature. In the mid-1800s, Colonel Fowler built this home, which is now Ramsey's Funeral Home.

WALLKILL RIVER BRIDGE, Franklin, N. J.

The road from Franklin to North Church went across the Wallkill River over this narrow stone bridge (called the Fowler Bridge) in the area known as the Junction. In 1928, due to the many railroad tracks and the looping Wallkill, the Viaduct, as it is known, was built from leftover railway materials and this bridge was put out of service; however, it still stands today. The riverbed just south of the Junction is a rich source of Indian relics. (Truran collection.)

SUSSEX COUNTY TRUST CO. & FRANKLIN THEATRE, FRANKLIN, N. J.

The Franklin Theater opened in 1914 with the play *The Chocolate Soldier*. It was touted to be the best theater between New York City and Pittsburgh. There was a roller-skating rink in the basement. To the left is the building that was Franklin's first bank. (Courtesy Michael Stefkovich.)

The musical comedy *Bimbo* was staged by the Phyllis Club in the Franklin Theater in April 1924. The Phyllis Club did a number of hugely successful community events. The club was named after Phyllis Treloar, a nurse who died helping the sick during the Spanish flu epidemic in 1919. The Phyllis Club operated for many years, and the name was later changed to the Wallkill Valley Woman's Club. (Samuel Harty Truran photograph.)

This early hotel was built after 1860 and before 1900 in the hamlet of Greenspot. It was known as Pollard Hotel, and perhaps Day & Puglia, before it was purchased as the company hotel by the New Jersey Zinc Company and named the Sterling Hotel. It was torn down in 1910 to make way for the new Palmer Mine and Mill complex.

The hotel was situated where the Time office remains today. A roadway ran along the front, down the hill, and to the north, dead-ending at Sterling Park, which then consisted of six homes near Mill and Sterling Streets. The Sterling House had an icehouse and a wooden stave water tower behind it. To the left is the Jeffrey House, which was another place for lodging the many miners and company visitors to the area. At the far left are several young men standing outside a small building that served as a post office. (Fred J. Stephens collection.)

The New Jersey Zinc Company general store was located across the street from the Sterling Hotel, in the hamlet of Greenspot. It was managed by the previous owner of the store, a man named McCarthy, who may have been the same McCarthy who had a general store in the now ghost town of Edison at the Ogden Mines atop Sparta Mountain. Here, one could purchase all kinds of groceries and dry goods. The railroad siding in the distance came across the dusty road and brought in coal and lumber to a shed in the rear, which housed a weigh scale. Twin bowling alleys were in the basement. The Nabe was torn down several years ago. Note the streetlight hanging from the building. Pictured in this 1902 scene are Tom Omaly, Fred Burns ("the usual Hancy store manager"), George Nestor, Fred Daily, Charles K. Clopper, Doc Hulshizer, and Ed Holly (deliveryman). (Richard Garrity collection.)

This interior view was taken after the company store moved across the street to the west into the brick building, which is still there today. The store was moved when the Palmer Shaft opened in 1910. Pictured are Harry Hardy (left) and John Kish. The store sold National Biscuit Company products from Hamburg's gristmill: Butter Thins, Lemon Snaps, vanilla wafers—names that sound as modern as today. (Sydney Hall collection.)

This is where we will take you.

This view shows the already extensive operations at Mill No. 2 below where the Palmer Shaft was to be located after 1912. The tracks at the Junction locality can be seen in the center. The Junction is the confluence of the New York, Susquehanna & Western, the Delaware, Lackawanna & Western, and the Lehigh & Hudson River Railroads. Other names associated with trackage here are the Sussex and Mine Hill Railroads. The Junction housed the New York, Susquehanna & Western station and the Lehigh & Hudson River tower. Just to the left were the Junction houses and a Hungarian bottler and bar known as Antalts. Jack Devine brought the first skip of ore up the Palmer Shaft in April 1910 and brought the last skip up on September 30, 1954. It was a sad day when the Franklin mine closed.

One of the separately owned and operated mines consolidated after 1898 was the Parker Mill and Shaft. It was located on the present firehouse grounds. Here, the new Ames and Wetherall separator was first used, an advance in mining techniques.

The raison d'être of Franklin was the mine. The many mines and owners were consolidated in 1898 into the New Jersey Zinc Company. They called in mining expert R. M. Catlin from South Africa, whose understudy was future president Herbert Hoover. Catlin made the mines a success story. The other mines and shafts were shut down, and the Palmer Shaft and

Mill complex operated as the main facility until closing in 1954. These views show how the complex looked. The importance of the New Jersey Zinc Company and the zinc-mining operations cannot be overstated. They made Franklin a world-class mining town. (Sydney Hall collection.)

This view looks eastward from atop the headframe of the Palmer Shaft at the Mill No. 2 complex c. 1914. The Parker plant stacks are still evident, although shutting down, and the company store is seen across Main Street in the old Greenspot hamlet. With the advent of mining here, the rail track to the shed in the back is gone. The new Quinn's Colonial Hotel stands across from where the Sterling House once stood.

One of the many benefits the New Jersey Zinc Company bestowed upon Franklin was a clubhouse, in the right foreground. The community house (later known as the Nabe) was moved down to the center of Greenspot, and this building became the company offices. In the right distance is the home built for R. M. Catlin, which included lodging for the chauffeur, because Catlin was deemed very important. When Catlin left the company, the house became bachelor quarters for men affiliated with the mine. In the left foreground left is the dormitory where other bachelors stayed. In the left distance, on top of the hill, was the mine superintendent's house, now known as the McCann House, which was also occupied by Ben Tillson and Walter Evans, who acted as superintendents.

The biggest day for Franklin was March 18, 1913, the day the community became the borough of Franklin. A big celebration was held in the middle of town near the company store, with many residents in attendance. (Sydney Hall collection.)

Quinn's Hotel, Franklin Furnace, N. J.

Joseph Patrick Quinn Sr., who was born in Hamburg and served as mayor of Franklin, became the manager for the Sterling Hotel, which was the company hotel c. 1900. R. M. Catlin of the New Jersey Zinc Company came to Quinn one day and stood in the lobby and said that the building would have to be torn down since the new Palmer Shaft was going to be driven right underfoot. So, Quinn built his own hotel across the street on property that is now a parking lot at the corner of Parker and Main Streets. The new hotel had steam heat and a bathroom on every floor. The basement contained the boiler and two large vat: one with whiskey and the other with beer—until Prohibition, of course. The small shack behind Quinn's is Weber's Barber Shop. Weber's son Joe continued to run the business in a shop on Main Street, just up the road to the left, until the 1980s. (Courtesy Franklin Mineral Museum.)

Quinn's Hotel Bar had to be torn down c. 1929 because it was sinking due to the shallow depth of the mine right under it. In this view, Kathleen Quinn Fleck is fourth from left, Marion Quinn Morrow is fifth from the left, and the man next to her is James Quinn, brother of Joseph Quinn Sr. The man on the right is likely George Piggery of Hamburg, who later visited the Quinns when they moved to Newton. Notice the calendar in the background, advertising insurance from T. D. Edsall (see the Hamburg section). (Courtesy Franklin Mineral Museum.)

96

This *c.* 1904 photograph was taken from the middle of the Greenspot locality, looking southward up Main Street toward the future location of the theater. After the opening of the Palmer complex, this area quickly grew from small wood frame one-story stores to large multiple-story buildings. (Courtesy Franklin Mineral Museum.)

A mere 15 to 20 years later, Franklin is a bustling mining town. Note the new brick company store on the left at the bottom of the hill. This was later a drugstore. (Courtesy Franklin Mineral Museum.)

This Fasolo family photograph from the late 1930s is a rare view of one of the earliest hamlets in the Franklin area: the Plains Settlement, named because of the flat and unwooded intervale as depicted in Haines's history. The famous gristmill used by Dr. Samuel Fowler is in the background. Here is where he perfected the use of zinc in white paint, a huge advancement for the 1820s. The family is standing approximately where the Dr. Samuel Fowler mansion was before it burned down in the mid-1800s. To the right can be seen the Fowler railroad bridge that still stands over the Wallkill River just beyond its confluence with the White Pond brook that passes under the mill. The mill was for grist and also was a fulling mill. It burned down on Christmas Eve 1944. Shown in this image are, from left to right, Lena Catone Tuberose, Augustine, Joseph, Tom, and sister Cattone. (Courtesy Frank Fasolo.)

The Franklin Hospital was erected in 1908 in response to a need that R. M. Catlin saw when he realized that an injured miner had to go to Paterson to be treated. Like many other amenities supplied by the New Jersey Zinc Company, the hospital added to the good feeling between the mining company and the town. The Franklin Hospital served the community well for over 70 years and its presence was integral to Franklin's past. Many births (including the author's, his brother's, and both his parents') took place here. The hospital building became eligible for listing on the New Jersey Register of Historic Places by the New Jersey Historical Commission in 2004. (Fred J. Stephens collection.)

The New Jersey Zinc Company supplied just about every need. In addition to the hospital, the company had a traveling nurse. Flora Laverie Hall makes the rounds in the Siberia section of town. Nurse Flora also covered the kindergarten at the Nabe and one on Spry Street (now named for John Wilton, who was killed in World War II.) (Sydney Hall collection.)

During World War I, a shortage of labor for the mines made the New Jersey Zinc Company look south of the border. Many Mexicans came to the Franklin-Ogdensburg area at this time, some jumping trains and others departing from the Pancho Villa war. This group of Chileans is being coached in soccer by Sydney Hall (left, standing), a Cornish immigrant who became the mine safety director. (Sydney Hall collection.)

In the early 1900s, about one quarter of all the miners were of Hungarian extraction, first-generation immigrants "just off the boat." Many of their descendants still live in the Franklin area. The Hungarians, as well as the Cornish, Mexican, Latvian, Russians, and others, brought their homeland customs with them. One highlight was the Hungarian Band, which played from c. 1905 to 1910, with Remus Kozma, and later with Matayas Kish and Stephen Bendes as leaders. The Hungarian church was moved from Edison (the old schoolhouse) to Evans Street. For many years now, the Franklin Band has been a regional mainstay in parades and at concerts. (Sydney Hall collection.)

Sterling Street in Franklin was built c. 1915 for company workers' housing. The area has been frequently referred to as Mexico, but in reality there were many Hungarians who lived here. At one time, the street was known by the residents as *a magyar utca,* "the Hungarian street," with ducks and chickens in the yards, some cows, and all-day pig roasts. The bungalows had four rooms, and the rent was $8 a month. At times, the tenant lived in the kitchen and the boarders lived in the other three rooms, with two beds for each and three persons per room on shifts. Prior to World War I, there was no electricity, gas, or plumbing. As did many other ethnics, these immigrants saved their paychecks and sent the money back to "the old country" to their wives, whom they often did not see for years. (Courtesy Sterling Hill Mine Museum.)

Shown is another set of bungalow-style houses built to the east, near the Hamburg Mountains. This area became known as Siberia because of the number of eastern Europeans who lived here. The Spry Street (John Wilton Street) area was also built about this time. Earlier, there were "flying cottages" here—homes on four blocks that were moved frequently to be near the mines and moved again as the mine expanded. Notice Route 23 in the foreground. Put in c. 1929, it was one of the first concrete two-lane highways. Just below the highway is the Mine Hill Railroad, which, to the right, goes to the old Parker Mill site and up to the Ding Dong, Trotter Shaft, and B. D. Simmons lumber company. (Sydney Hall collection.)

Named after the company from which the plans came, the Better Home section of Franklin was built c. 1927 and was where many of the English lived. Again, this was company housing built to accommodate the constantly growing population to work in the mines. This modern development had a separate garage, some concrete roads with curbs, storm drains, sewers, fire hydrants, concrete sidewalks on both sides—quite a modern development. (Courtesy Sterling Hill Mine Museum.)

Shown is the old main street in Franklin Furnace. At the beginning of the 20th century, the main street in Franklin Furnace was High Street. In fact, before 1900 there were pastures where Main Street north now is. The post office and many stores were on High Street. The parade was along High Street. Once the town was incorporated, the borough hall was moved to this location at the southeast corner of High and Parker Streets. Note the World War I field artillery guarding the entrance, left over from the mock battle performed in Shuster Park and brought in on a rail car. Also note the woman walking along the Mine Hill Railroad behind the borough hall. All buildings were torn down in later years as the mine tunneling, which was directly under this area, created cave-ins. (Courtesy John Kolic.)

Post Office, Franklin, N. J.

Just south of the borough hall was the post office. This view looks northwestward toward the intersection of High and Junction Streets. The person serving as postmaster changed as the political administration in Washington changed. This is only one of several locations for the post office at the time. It also was in Greenspot, just west of here, in a very small building, and at the McCarthy New Jersey Zinc Company general store.

High Street, Franklin, N. J.

Looking westward at the intersection of High and Junction Streets, this view shows Fogelson's Dry Goods. Many of the merchants were Hungarian Jews, such as Isadore Fischgrund, Emanuel Weiss, Morris Grossman, the Markovitzes, the Mindlins, and the Honigs. There was also Perlee's Store (in the north end of town), catering more to the English, and Riggio's, Topel's, Simp's, Demario's, and other local markets. Just beyond on the left is the Gunderman Theater, where "the flickers" were shown, before electricity, with an acetylene gas lamp. As the picture dimmed, the viewers would say, "Sam, the gas is getting low."

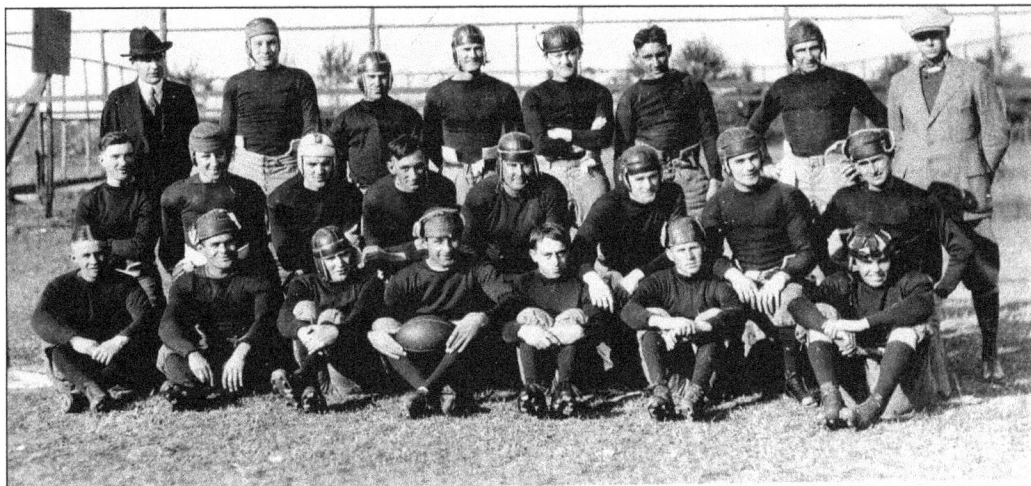

Franklin Football Team
Left to Right - Top Row - G. W. Laurie, Manager; T, C, O'Neill, H. W. Fisher, D. Cowdrick, A. Korves, C. Paddock, E. Corroll, R.L. McCann, Coach
2ns Row - J. Glynn, Wm. McEntee, F. Stephens, R. Paddock, P Lanterman, F.Flynn, J. Devine, W. Donahue
Bottom Row - R. Lent, A. Donnelly, R. Bailey, S. Paddock, G. Houyoux, H. Fletcher, A. Wilson

Franklin was always known for having a tough group of men and sports teams that were hard to beat. This team from 1921 precedes the Franklin Miners of the 1930s and 1940s, who were known as winners throughout the East. (Fred J. Stephens collection.)

103

Franklin's outstanding citizens

Fowler Family
Dr. Samuel Fowler (1779-1844).
Combined science to the geology, business to the mining, world recognition to the treasures of Franklin. Franklin's greatest citizen.

- Physician who grew an interest in science and also business
- Considered one of the leading citizens of northern NJ.
- To Hamburg in 1800 as a physician
- purchase Mine Hill in 1820 with John O. Ford, eventually owning it all by 1817.
- Married Rebecca Ogden after his first wife, Ann Thomson, died.
- Later he acquired Sterling Mine
- Spread the word of Franklin around the world
- Served in the NJ Senate
- Congressman to Washington 1833-1837.
  Colonel Samuel Fowler (1818-1865)
    - Civil War colonel, commanded the 15th NJ Regiment (including these three companies: D from Lafayette, I from Newton, and K from Hardyston)
    - Served, albeit only a few days, in the State Legislature 1864

Munson Family
Family moved to area at an early time
Israel was born here 1771
Asa (pictured) there about 1880
Samuel Munson
11/4/1876-5/12/1961 owned and operated general store
1913-1918-State Senator
1914-1959-operated the Franklin Theatre
1919-1961-Bank Director Sussex County Trust Company, President 1944-60
State Senator and tax collector for Hardyston Twp

Littell Family
- Late 1600's to Sussex County
- Aaron had a farm in White Lake area
- Watson: to Franklin, Franklin House (ca 1900-1914), beer bottling (ca 1900-1920), Franklin Town Council 1913
- Alfred Beattie (AB "Bike"):b. 1903, ice\gas\appliance in 1920-30's, Assemlby 1922
- Robert E.: Assembly 1967-1990, Senate: 1990-2003+
- Allison McHose: Assembly 2003+

Shown are some of the prominent citizens of Franklin.

Robert M. Catlin (1853-1934) *"The Man that Saved Franklin"*

- Superintendent at the Franklin and Sterling Hill mine plants for 15 years
- engineer in Nevada for 20, South Africa for 11.
- When in S. Africa, a junior engineer under him was Herbert Hoover (first Stanford grad class)
- Filled the many unused mining holes
- Established a humane community
- Began process for Franklin Hospital
- Water system
- Paved streets
- Founded a community house
- Arranged for bank and general store

Chief Herbert C. Irons *"rode in on horseback and brought law and order to the mining town"*

- Came in 1915 from the Canal Zone just after Franklin's incorporation, when it was a rough and tumble town
- put over 30 lawbreakers into state prison in cleaning up
- hauled in a murderer in 1921 in the famous "Cat Swamp Robbery"
- remembered even today as "a cop 24 hours a day"

The Immigrant Miners

1850-60s   Irish iron workers, occupying "bed bug row" of many family row houses.

1895-1915 Eastern Europeans (mostly Hungarians), up to 25% of the NJZC workforce.

1905-1915 Cornish miners and experienced mining engineers

1915-1920 Mexican and Chilean workers

Pictured here are more Franklin citizens.

Here is Franklin's last undefeated team, the baseball team of 1944. In that era, baseball was the national sport. A few years later, Franklin's own Billy Glynn played first base for the Cleveland Indians in the World Series. From left to right are the following: (first row) Richie Sparnon, Tony Hlavka, Bill May, Monk Stevens, Willie Truran, and Carl Zucknovich; (second row) Abe Wexler, Ken Manuel, "Wild Bill" Parachmichuk, Bill Sabo, and Lou Kota. Jay Burd had already headed off to war, and coach Reg Purdy is not in the picture.

Franklin was part of Hardyston Township until 1913. There was a high school in Hamburg, also part of the same township, as well as one in Newton. Franklin opened a vocational technical school in 1915. A junior high was added in 1922 and a senior high in 1927. In 1959, an addition was finished, including a new gymnasium, auditorium, and six classrooms. For many years into the 1980s, Franklin was the only school in New Jersey having classes for kindergarten all the way through grade 12 in the same building. (Courtesy Franklin Historical Society.)

Four

HAMBURG

The Children's Town, home of the Gingerbread Castle and the Windsor Lime Kilns.

Hamburg was one of the first local areas settled by the Europeans. Sketchy references indicate that William Gould, Thomas Wright, and Isaac and William Titsworth were early landowners. Joseph Walling (or Wallens) arrived here *c.* 1749 and built a log cabin, probably a mill, and later a frame dwelling at the crossroads of the King's Highway (Route 94) and the path northwest. That northwest path was later known as the Deckertown Pike, a continuation of the Hamburg Paterson Turnpike that was created during the turnpike era that began *c.* 1804. The road is present-day Route 23. Tracts of land at this early time were purchased or leased from large landowners who in many cases were grantees or buyers of the original land patents and had very large holdings. Other later large landowners in the Hamburg area included Lewis Morris, Joseph Sharpe, and Martin Ryerson. Morris was a signer of the Declaration of Independence and colonial governor of New York, and owned land and a plantation named Morrisania (in what is now the Bronx) while owning farmland in Sussex County known as Morrisvale (north of Hamburg). The land was later owned by the related Lawrence family from Philadelphia, who built a home near the Wallkill bridge and later built close by this on higher ground the mansion Claremont in 1794. The Lawrence family helped shape Hamburg in a number of ways. Industrious in his ventures, Sharpe (or Sharp) built farther south along the Wallkill River. Here, the river was dammed up and at least two iron forges were built and later a gristmill. Although it changed hands several times, the gristmill eventually became so prosperous that it succeeded all of the other gristmills in the area. It in fact became a leading provider of flour for the region and was an integral part of the large Nabisco brands (which acquired the Uneeda brand) that to this day retains the Wheatsworth cracker from Hamburg's mill.

Hamburg and its citizens participated in all of the nation's conflicts. During the Revolutionary War, the Continental army marched through the important crossroads of Hamburg. Gen. George Washington's troops are believed to have encamped in 1778 and 1781 on travel between New York State and points south during the conflict. Washington is said to have stopped at the Walling residence on his travels, and tradition has it that Martha Washington stayed there and that Walling provided the troops with flour from his mill. There is said to have been a blockhouse from the Revolution that was manned by local men of the 2nd Regiment of the Sussex militia, who practiced on the flat area behind Main Street. Defeated British troops of Gen. John Burgoyne's army passed through under guard along the King's Highway. Hamburg men also served during the War of 1812, defending Cape May from the British. A cannon was to have been kept at Hamburg at one time. Many of the men of Hamburg served in the Civil War. Alanson Austin Haines, son of the governor of New Jersey, was a chaplain in the 15th Regiment, made up largely of Hardyston men. During the Civil War, as well as the Revolution and the War of 1812, companies made up regiments, and these companies usually were completely filled with men from the same towns. Thus, soldiers served with their neighbors, and when many losses occurred during a major battle, such as Fredericksburg, they often included a number of men from one town.

Hamburg has always been home to a several industries. Starting with Wallings mill, the Hamburg Iron Works, and then Sharp's gristmill and ironworks, two sawmills, a tannery, two lime works and a cement plant, a creamery, and a very large paper manufacturer, Hamburg earned a reputation as a mill town. The Main Street section had hardware, pharmacy, milk creamery, banking, and coal-handling businesses before neighboring towns did. The Gingerbread Castle remains a destination for many.

Prominent Hamburg citizens include Robert A. Linn, Thomas D. Edsall, Judge Skinner, Marin Ryerson, Reeve Harden, Col. Joseph E. Edsall, Benjamin Hamilton, Dr. L'Hommedieu, Dr. William Linn (of Linn Hospital), Abe Rude, Drs. Jackson and Thomas Pellett, and Dr. Updegrove.

Hamburg's population remained stable from the early 1800s to the mid-1900s. It has been a major crossroads in the county and remains so today.

Hamburg is known as the Children's Town because of the presence of the Gingerbread Castle. The area was known at various times as Wallings and Sharpsboro, and Jesse Potts' Hamburg Iron Works. The name Hamburg took hold permanently when Thomas Lawrence helped establish the post office in 1795 near the Hamburg Iron Works.

Hamburg has always served as host to well-trodden crossroads. All of the major thoroughfares at one time were Indian paths, later worn by settlers moving in and trading. Route 94 was known in Colonial times as the King's Highway and was used, ironically, by Gen. George Washington in moving his troops through Hamburg in 1779 and 1782. The present Route 23 had in the early 1800s been known as the Paterson-Hamburg Turnpike, which came over the Hamburg Mountains from Pequannock and into Hardystonville and Upper Hamburg, and was joined with the Hamburg Road from Franklin Furnace. Incorporated in 1920, the town is today a prosperous and growing community with state Routes 23 and 94 as central forces.

Notably, the lime kilns were recognized in June 2004 by the state for their historic value. A land swap allows the state to preserve the kilns, and the state historic preservation office has called them "the most historically significant kilns in the mid-Atlantic region."

Some of the hamlets in Hamburg and the environs include the following:

Pennyrock
Bank's Development
Heritage Lakes–the Quarry
Cloud Crest
Wheatsworth
Main Street
Winding Brook
Oak Point
Hamburg Village
Upper Hamburg

N. Y. S. & W. Depot, Hamburg, N. J.

Shown is Hamburg station. The railroad was established here in 1872 as the Midland Railroad extended north from Franklin. That line went toward Middletown and later turned into the New York, Susquehanna & Western. A second line was the Lehigh & Hudson Railroad. Coal was a major product brought into this station. Note the old crossing sign. There was another small station a mile south in Upper Hamburg at the paper mill serviced by the Lehigh & Hudson.

Just up the hill from the railroad station is the National Hotel of Hamburg, on the southwest corner of Wallkill Avenue and Orchard Street. This hotel was also known as the Simpson House or Smith Simpson Hotel. It began operation about the time of the railroads, in the early 1870s. The original hotel was destroyed by fire in 1903 and was rebuilt by Dymock & Son in 1906, with many Victorian features. After years of disuse, the hotel's remaining foundation was covered in 1957 and became the site of the Hamburg post office until c. 2001, when the post office moved to the Governor Haines Square and finally to the old Harden Garage site.

This is the home of Joseph Walling (or Wallens), one of Hamburg's earliest known settlers. He is said to have arrived c. 1749 and purchased 3,000 acres from the proprietors of New Jersey, and built a log cabin. The Walling holdings bordered those of Joseph Sharp and the Lawrence estate. Walling was a tanner by trade and, c. 1750, constructed the first frame house, which at the time, was known as the finest home in the village. On his way south in 1779, George Washington is believed to have stopped at the Walling house when his troops encamped on the Lawrence farm near the present-day Wallkill Valley High School. He likely stopped here again on his way north in 1782 for at least some cider or tea, as Walling was related to the Bairds who had a tavern in Warwick, where it was well documented that Washington visited. Other notables in the Wallkill Valley resided in this home: Martin Ryerson, who married to Rhoda Hull; Robert A. Linn, who married Elizabeth Ryerson; Dr. Samuel Fowler of Franklin; and Gov. Daniel Haines's brother, Stephen Haines. The house was destroyed by fire and replaced in 1859 by the well-known Edsall House, which was razed several years before the Hardyston National Bank, in 1953.

Just southwest of the train station, along the King's Highway, is Claremont. The Morris family had a Colonial plantation known as Morrisania in New York, just north of Manhattan. Gov. Lewis Morris owned land in Sussex County, including the Morrisvale farm. Morris was signer of the Declaration of Independence, colonial governor of New York, and an early proprietor of New Jersey. After the American Revolution, the Lawrence family bought property from the related Morris family. Claremont was the family estate of the Lawrence family. Thomas Lawrence of Hamburg was born here. This mansion and surrounding estate swept from the Wallings settlement at the crossroads down to Sharpsboro to the present-day Gingerbread Castle area, northward toward the Papakating Cemetery area (a very early Baptist meetinghouse is said to have stood near the mansion and then to have been moved to where Morrisvale was, up near Papakating) and westward toward North Church in Hardyston, ultimately including about 800 acres. Claremont, built in 1841 to replace an earlier mansion, was named after the Lawrence family home in the Philadelphia area. Claremont was located on higher ground than the original structure referred to as the Lawrence Mansion.

This view looks southeastward. A horse and wagon back into the store for loading. They are picking up goods from John Linn's, later Reeve Harden's Hamburg Hardware. Note the telegraph sign on the right at the Linn pharmacy. Dirt roads make for muddy streets, and the elevated wooden or concrete platforms certainly help in bad weather. The so-called Brick Block at one time had a bowling alley and billiard tables on the first floor and a dance hall and movie theater on the second floor.

This view shows Charles Linn's pharmacy and the Hardyston National Bank, which was formed in 1906. (Courtesy Antique Photo Store.)

This 1909 northwestward view was taken looking backward on the way up the short hill to the town center. At the end of Main Street is the Edsall house. This prime property was destroyed by fire and replaced in 1859. This Edsall house was then replaced by the bank that T. D. Edsall was instrumental in founding, known as the Hardyston National Bank. This Edsall lot is near the northwest corner of the Routes 23 and 94. (A. J. Bloom photograph; courtesy Antique Photo Store.)

The Ajax Drug Store was owned by C. H. Linn, inventor of two medicines: Ajax, a cough medicine with liquor, and Bjax, a cough medicine with whiskey. Linn sold writing paper, pencils, candy, and seeds. He also sold violins to the Hungarian and Welsh miners from Franklin. He was most famous for his ice cream, which was made of custard that he cooked from products of local farmers and ice from the pond behind his house, located on Vernon Avenue (Route 94). (Courtesy Antique Photo Store.)

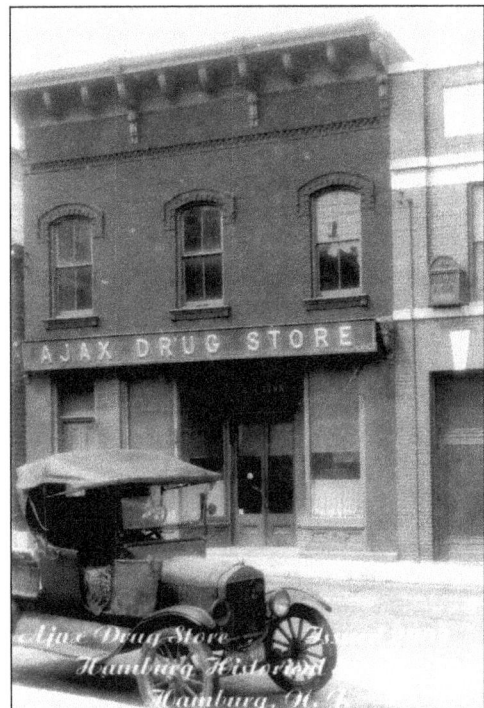

Hamburg's outstanding citizens

Thomas Lawrence Sr. came to Hamburg from Philadelphia in the 1700's. His son, known as Thomas Lawrence of Hamburg, of whom we speak of here, resided in the family mansion and estate known as Claremont. The vast land holdings include the present site of the Wallkill Regional High School where George Washington's troops encamped in 1779. Lawrence is credited with establishing a post office in town and development of the turnpike. He may be credited with the adoption of the name of Hamburg. The name had an additional "h" at the end from at least 1827 to 1894.

Governor Daniel Haines (1801-1877) is Hamburg's most famous citizen. He was born in NYC as the son of a successful business man, Elias Haines. Both parents were patriots during the Revolution. His mother was Mary Ogden, a person we have spoken of in Ogdensburg's story; and Mary's brother was also NJ governor. Haines graduated from the College of NJ in 1820 and studied law under Thomas Ryerson, and became an attorney in 1823 and practiced in Hamburg. He became State Senator in 1839, and in 1843 was chosen by his party to serve as governor, and then was elected governor in 1847 and then again in 1850. In 1852 he became a Supreme Court Justice for 2 seven year terms, was outstanding in the local Presbyterian Church. On his death all NJ flags flew at half-mast.

Dr. Joseph Couse was born in 1841 in Frankford Township. He was a school teacher who then served as a private in the Civil War in the 15th Regiment of the NJ Volunteers, Company H. By 1865 he became a captain of Company I. He served as with General Sherman in the March to the Sea campaign. The prominent Couse House was later razed for the present home of the Fire House and Municipal Building.

Richard E. Edsall was a prominent business man in Hamburg, member of several business interests in and outside of town. He donated land where the Episcopal Church has stood, and had built and resided in the Edsall dwelling at the crossroads.

Shown are some prominent Hamburg citizens.

114

Originally, this was a general store. Here, Coe Smith sold a wide variety of merchandise and even displayed a coconut from Florida in 1919 for those who had never seen one. The Hamburg Department Store was opened in 1922 by Barnet Lazarus, a Russian Jew from New York City. Farmers bought their dry goods from him since they did not have the time to travel by train to Paterson because their cows needed to be milked twice a day. In the late 1940s, this building became Hamburg Liquor, operated by Frank Hirsh, who came from Franklin. His brother Nate Hirsh operated the meat market on Main Street at about the same time. This building is located on the southwest corner of the intersection of Routes 23 and 94. (Courtesy Antique Photo Store.)

The Chardavoyne Building was located near the southeast corner of the intersection of Routes 23 and 94 at Vernon Avenue, where it heads toward McAfee and Vernon. It was built c. 1900 by I. D. Chardavoyne, who once served as Sussex County sheriff. Until 1933, the main floor was used as a millinery shop, first operated by Chardavoyne's wife. It then became the Hamburg post office. The second floor of the building was the Chardavoyne residence, and the third floor served as the town meeting place and headquarters for several lodges. It was commonly referred to as the Lodge Hall. It was torn down for the mini-mall that is now on the site. (Courtesy Antique Photo Store.)

Pausing in front of the Chardavoyne Building for a picture are a couple—likely T. D. Edsall and his wife—returning home from a breezy ride in their buggy. (Courtesy Harvey Barlow.)

Hamburg Historical Society
Issued November 2003

The Hamburg Hotel
Hamburg, N.J.

This old inn, the Hamburgh House, was on the northeast corner of the crossroads of Route 23 and Route 94. Research shows that it was likely built by Robert A. Linn in 1837 or earlier. It was remodeled c. 1872 in the Victorian style by its proprietor, James K. Smith. At the beginning of the 20th century, he was described as being "the best looking man in Hamburg . . . wearing a Greeley hat." The hotel was billed as "the finest resort in Northern New Jersey." Note the bandstand in the center of the intersection. Here, the Hamburg Cornet Band played on Saturday nights. (Courtesy Dr. Marion Wood.)

Land for a school was deeded as early as 1799 by Joseph and William Sharp, and Hamburg School District was recognized within the Hardyston Township School District in 1851. The grammar school was built c. 1880 and expanded in 1894. Called the White Building, it had white clapboards and green shutters outside and oiled floors within. Located on the same site as the present school complex, the building was torn down in 1963. An early academy was located across from the Baptist church at the rear of the blacksmith's Main Street property. A later one, the Hamburg Academy, is said to have existed from c. 1851 to 1899 and to have started as a privately owned school (1851 marking the beginning of public financing of the school). Daniel Haines was one of the leaders in promoting public education, even on the local level. (Courtesy Angeline Truran Hoppler.)

A school bell from 1886 is displayed in the present school, and one that replaced it c. 1924 is in the municipal hall. The bell could be heard all around Hamburg. It was rung after lunch and also sometimes after recess to call the children back to continue the day's work. After 1908, Hamburg acted as the high school for a large area. It was the second of only two secondary schools in Sussex County, the other being in Newton, which graduated four men in 1905. Hamburg graduated two students in 1907, Florence Farber and Annette Dennis. This is the date the alumni uses but maybe some graduated earlier in 1905 or 1906. The high school existed earlier in order for the students to complete the course of study. Mrs. Farber recently passed away at age 100-plus. The horse-drawn school bus carried students from Vernon, Glenwood, Rudeville, and greater Hardyston Township. Some came by rail from Ogdensburg and Franklin, leaving before dawn on the back of a milk train. Motorized buses were used, beginning c. 1918, with the Republica, featuring wooden seats and oilcloth windows. (Courtesy Antique Photo Store.)

This is a view of the first brick school building, with the older wood frame so-called White Building behind it. The brick school was built in 1912 by Jonathan Dymock & Sons, who built many of the homes in Hamburg. The high school began in one room on the upper floor of the frame building in 1905 and moved to its own building, Hamburg High School, in 1912.

The last graduating class of Hamburg High School was the class of 1962. The school is still in use for primary through eighth-grade classes. From 1963 to 1984, students went to Franklin High School to complete their four years of secondary school. Today, the Wallkill Regional High School serves the same Hardyston Township of the late 1800s: Franklin, Ogdensburg, Hamburg, and Hardyston. (Courtesy Dr. Marion Wood.)

The Hamburg Baptist Church is the oldest of the several churches in Hamburg. Church records date back to 1798, but a "preaching house" location is not known—perhaps on the hill behind the Lawrence Mansion and, later, near the Papakating Deckertown Cemetery to serve the larger Wantage membership. Besides the Wantage congregation, Rev. Thomas Teasdale organized the First Baptist Church of Hamburg in Vernon in 1798. The church was moved to Hamburg in 1811, as it was closer to many of its members. In 1814, Martin Ryerson donated this land and that of the adjoining cemetery, and the church was incorporated in 1835. The building was destroyed by fire on January 29, 1936.

The rebuilt church on the same location was made of brick, as was the Hamburg National Hotel. Rev. Robert L. Wood stated, "We have never missed a Sunday of worship after the fire until the new church was built." It has been noted that baptisms took place outside, mainly in the Wallkill River—even in winter, when the ice was cut in the shape of a human.

The Presbyterian church in the Wallkill Valley began in Robert Ogden's home as early as 1780. The Hardyston church was organized in 1786, with the building being at the "head of the Wallkill" in present-day Sparta. Before 1918, services took place in the Carey Meeting House (the present-day Hardyston Cemetery), and in 1831, in the North Church site just down the hill. Services were held in the Hamburg area, first, in the school prior to 1814, and then, along with Baptists, in a meetinghouse on land donated by Martin Ryerson, the present site of the Hamburg Baptist Church. Bethany Chapel, the stone edifice shown here, was built in 1869 on land donated by former governor Daniel Haines. Alanson Austin Haines, son of the governor, was a well-known pastor and local historian of the mid-1800s.

PRESBYTERIAN CHURCH, HAMBURG, N.J.
Built 1869

The Episcopal church, known as the Church of the Good Shepherd, was built in 1869 on land donated by the Edsall family, heir to the Robert L. Linn property. Due to changes in construction plans, the first church service was not held until June 3, 1874. The congregation moved north of town in 1987. However, this building still stands on Route 23.

Shown is the Edsall House *c.* 1905, when still occupied by the Edsall family. The tower was not part of the original structure but was added later and used as a maid's room and office space.

This Georgian Colonial Governor Haines Mansion was built as home by Joseph Sharpe (later spelled Sharp). Caleb and Isaacher Rude were involved in the construction. In 1823, Daniel Haines acquired the home, and it stayed in his family for over a century. In 1932, Bennett's Wheatsworth Inn opened a restaurant here. Flagstone walks and old Colonial-style gardens and ponds with giant goldfish served many weddings. (Courtesy Antique Photo Store.)

Several disastrous fires occurred in the early 1900s. One of them was the 1909 broom factory fire that took with it several buildings owned by Reeve Harden on the lower portion of Wallkill Avenue. One week after that fire, the fire department came into being, on December 23, 1909. The earliest fire alarms were sounded by banging on a wheel from an old steam locomotive. The first fire truck was a hook-and-ladder, which was stored on Main Street under the new Hardyston National Bank. From 1918 to 1961, the firehouse was later located in the former Ellsworth Adams garage on Wallkill Avenue. (Courtesy Hamburg Historical Society.)

The Hamburg Cornet Band, the earliest organized band in town, poses on the steps of the National Hotel. Very popular, there were four known cornet bands in the county in the late 1800s. The Hamburg Cornet Band gave regular Saturday night concerts at the bandstand in front of the Hamburg Inn that stood from 1896 to the late 1920s. There were many local dance bands, such as Rube Kimble's Blue Bird Orchestra of the 1920s, and Rube's Ramblers. There also was the Westervelt Orchestra. The Teabout family, including members of the Piggery family, played banjo, guitar, jew's harp, and mouth organ for gatherings. (Courtesy Hamburg Historical Society.)

At the south end of Main Street was the Harden Garage, one of Reeve Harden's several businesses. From left to right are Bill Lozaw, Pat Jensen, Rembert Doland, Merritt Doland, Verner Cole, Gladys Van Syckle, Abe Rude, and Lester McPeek. In the early years, the garage sold Reos, Fords, and other makes of automobiles. Later, it became a Buick dealer. (A. J. Bloom photograph, 1925; courtesy Antique Photo Store.)

Sharpsboro was located was in the Gingerbread Castle Road area and included the 550-acre Joseph Edsall farm. The Sharpe family came here as early as 1751 and began iron-mining operations. The stone mill, built in 1808, is the oldest industrial building still standing in Hamburg. The mill took water from the Wallkill River via a flume and sluiceway to an overshot waterwheel. The mill was at one time four stories high. Here, farmers brought their grain for processing into flour, usually for the farmer to take home. This mill worked with buckwheat and wheat—very successful operations. In 1921, F. M. Bennett Biscuit Company, later Wheatsworth Mills, owned the site and produced the famous Wheatsworth stone-ground crackers, which are still sold today under the Nabisco brands. A Uneeda Bakers sales stand for Wheatsworth can be seen in the Franklin general store photograph. (Samuel Harty Truran collection.)

Shown is the Gingerbread Castle, Hamburg's famous landmark. In 1928, Wheatsworth Mills owner Francis H. Bennett desired to re-create the fanciful costumes and sets he had seen in his Manhattan viewing of Engelbert Humperdink's opera *Hansel and Gretel*. He enlisted the highly respected architect, book illustrator, and set designer Joseph Urban, who had done the Tsar Bridge in St. Petersburg and exhibit buildings for Austria in Paris in 1900 and the St. Louis Fair in 1904. Bennett told Urban to "make your greatest work, an everlasting monument to you." Bennett's vision, coupled with his profession as a baker, produced much concrete resembling gingerbread dripping from roofs with icing, crackers, cookies, and plum pudding. At the castle, which is still open to visitors during the summer months, local teenage guides, dressed as Hansels and Gretels, tell stories and nursery rhymes. The boys wear green or brown felt Peter Pan hats with feathers (also sold in the store, along with pennants). They warn against touching the gingerbread lest it turn to stone, which, of course, has been tried many times and found to be true. (Courtesy Dr. Marion Wood.)

Many of the characters at the Gingerbread Castle come from *Grimm's Fairy Tales*. Snow White, Little Red Riding Hood, Little Miss Muffett, and the Lady in the Shoe are among these representations.

The *Fairy Land Limited*, also known as the *Gingerbread Castle Limited*, was launched with the hammering of a golden spike at a ribbon-cutting ceremony in May 1955. The train ran on a half-mile-long circular track that crossed water diverted from the Wallkill River, with a young engineer in a hat and scarf sounding the horn to the pleasure of many a youngster. (Courtesy Dr. Marion Wood.)

In this view from Motorcycle Hill, Upper Hamburg village is seen at the southern end of town. Much of Upper Hamburg was built up and depended upon the paper mill that was located downhill a short walk away (just out of sight below the hill from which this picture was taken). Company housing can be seen on the right on what is today Urban Street, named after Urban, who was instrumental designing the Gingerbread Castle. (Courtesy Harvey Barlow.)

The Paper Mill, Hamburg, N. J.

The paper mill grew out of a site on the Wallkill River where the Hamburg Furnace was until 1850, and later a sawmill and steam bending works by Peloubet & Sons c. 1873. As more power was needed, the dam was raised in height, and this also increased the size of the paper mill pond upstream behind it. The paper mill came into being shortly thereafter. This operation was owned by the Sparks Manufacturing Company and, later, the Union Waxed Paper and Parchment Company. This large operation produced a variety of products including newspaper, wrapping, and bag paper. The Wallkill, with the aid of the dam, was able to produce at least 250 horsepower with Whalen turbine waterwheels. The boiler produced steam and heated the pulp, and was rated at 50 horsepower. Paper is still made the same way today as it was then. An additional step was making waxed paper out of this material. The paper mill pond is in the left foreground, with the dam in the mid-ground. Downstream in the distance, part of the plant spanned the Wallkill. The upper track at the far right is the Lehigh & Hudson River Railroad, which winds to the right just beyond the plant, where Route 23 is today, and up to Warwick. The lower track at the right is the New York, Susquehanna & Western Railroad, which goes to the Hamburg station and then toward Sussex and up to New York State through Wantage. Several lower tracks service the mill. (Truran collection.)

This view of the paper mill complex was taken looking southward. The dam can be seen, with the white water flowing between the trees, to the right. (A. J. Bloom photograph; courtesy Antique Photo Store.)

126

Stoll's Pond is in Hardystonville near the edge of Hamburg, Hardyston, and Franklin, at the foot of the mountainous pathway of the Hamburg Turnpike. Hardystonville in the mid-1800s had a blacksmith shop, a gristmill, two carpentry shops, a store, a schoolhouse, lodgings, and a number of residences including no less than eight Edsall family farms. (Courtesy Harvey Barlow.)

The Windsor Lime Kilns were located south of the paper mill and east of the river, in the woods around the corner on the rail lines. The kilns are one of Hamburg's greatest archaeological treasures. They were named for the operations begun in 1876 and lasting into the early 20th century, also associated with Sayres & Vanderhoof. Limestone was mined in at the Windsor Quarry (now Crystal Springs, in Hardyston) and the Atlas Quarry (now Heritage Lakes, in Hamburg) and brought down the hill along the stream from Upper Hamburg by means of a narrow-gauge railroad track. The Windsor Lime Kilns produced as much as 100,000 barrels of lime per year, much of it transported by the Lehigh & Hudson River Railroad. Other lime works were in the Hamburg area were the Wallkill Cement and Lime (on the Lehigh & Hudson River beyond Hamburg Junction just before the present Route 23) and the White Rock Lime and Cement near McAfee. At one time a narrow-gauge railway took ore from the Windsor Quarry directly to White Rock. The Wallkill Valley here was extremely rich in the limestone that, when burned to lime, was used as flux in the smelting of iron ore found in the area. Later, this lime was sent in huge quantities to western Pennsylvania to the Bethlehem Steel. In obtaining the high-temperature fires required for both the iron furnaces and for the making of lime, much charcoal was produced and used. Thus, in old photographs it is evident that there are very few trees on the landscape of the Wallkill Valley. Into the 20th century, the Atlas Branch of the Lehigh & Hudson River went to the quarries in Hardystonville and transported the ore to a place near the Palmer Mill in Franklin to catch the main line.

This aerial view of Hamburg was taken looking northward from Upper Hamburg along Route 23 in 1963. When compared with images from the early 1900s, it shows how much the landscape had changed by the 1960s.

The huge elm tree was likely located on the left side of Vernon Avenue just before the road heads out of town toward McAfee. Another large old elm tree grew on Route 94, the old King's Highway that winds past the Claremont Mansion, where George Washington's troops are believed to have slept in 1779. These trees are now gone. Their passing is symbolic of the lost times recalled only in memories and stored in images such as this. (Courtesy Antique Photo Store.)

www.ingramcontent.com/pod-product-compliance
Lightning Source LLC
Chambersburg PA
CBHW050623110426
42813CB00007B/1704